30 YEARS CARRYING THE BAG

FINANCIAL WHOLESALING DURING THE 80's, 90's, and 2000's

James Patrick Naughton

30 YEARS CARRYING THE BAG

FINANCIAL WHOLESALING DURING the '80s, the '90s
and the 2000s

www.KeyPublishingCompany.com

LinkedIn

Facebook

Printed in the United States of America

Cover designed by Arthur Garceau, Print World, Owner-
Raoul Holzinger, Post Road, North Kingstown, RI

ISBN | 978-0-9858377-5-4

Preface

This book is for Juniors and Seniors looking for a unique career upon graduation, for new Financial Wholesalers, and anyone interested in a Financial Wholesaler's life. Finally, it represents my thanks to everyone who contributed to my success as a 'Billion Dollar Wholesaler.'

Many years ago, I recall reading about Life Coaches suggesting that one way to become successful in a particular field was to find and read about someone who has already done so.

One example that stood out, was during military training for the Expert Marksman designation,
The coach would have new recruits note and copy every action that their best Expert Marksmen exhibited and have the soldiers emulate them. (Their breathing, their timing, their posture, the way they slowly pulled the trigger and so on). This method of training was new to the military, however the success ratio improved dramatically from the older training methods. They not only created more Expert Marksmen, but did so at a faster pace.

With this book, I try to give my readers that type of information with the use of actual stories depicting how I did the job. It's true it's a different era today, however the basics stay the same. You will need to adapt to the yearly changes of the job and industry, but thats the same for any career.

Note: If you read my story *Jump in and start swimming,* you will see some overlap as I discuss aspects of my career for college seniors, which I pulled from the outline for this book in 2010. In addition, my career experiences are shown in *Relationships open doors*, and some chapters in my most recently published, *The Greatest*, were also borrowed from this book's outline. Those three books and my childhood story, *WHATEVER HAPPENED TO PECORDS? HEAVEN SENT* also comprises *My How to Live Forever Series,*' designed to encourage my Baby Boomer generation to write down a piece of theirs or their family's history and preserve it, FOREVER!

Prologue

I begin discussing my wholesaling career towards the end and will revisit the beginning later in the book. I decided on this because the end of 2003 began what would become the most challenging period in my nearly 30-year career. Don't worry; you will read what it was like as an Internal Wholesaler in the early 80s and then my experience as an External Wholesaler in the 90s and 2000s. For college students and those new to Financial Wholesaling, I describe my daily activities and how to become a Wholesaler toward the end of the book. In addition, you can scroll down the Chapter list if you would like to start at the beginning of my career or later.

Financial Wholesalers are responsible for bringing (wholesaling) their firm's products to advisors and providing information (selling) on why the advisors (their clients) would want to place these products in their client's investment portfolios. This brief outline of a wholesaler's function is essential when looking into the industry for the first time.

Contents

Chapter I

2004, After the 'Close' — Meeting With Merrill Lynch Advisors

It's about 3:30 pm in late spring 2004, and I am at the popular restaurant, Max's Downtown, Hartford, Connecticut. After the 'close' (the stock market always closes at 4 pm), the meeting with Merrill Lynch Advisors, upstairs in City Place on Asylum Avenue, is about to begin. My speaker this afternoon is Thomas Melendez, an International Money Manager for my former firm MFS. (MFS – Massachusetts Financial Services. America's oldest mutual fund company). Steve Abrams, the restaurant manager, is walking in and waiving, calling my name, "Hey Jimmy, how's everything in North Kingstown?''

His father owned a hardware store on Main Street, East Greenwich, Rhode Island, next town over from mine, where he worked while attending college. I have been a Financial Wholesaler for Massachusetts Financial Services 'MFS' since 1987. I know everybody in New England and many all over New York. Melendez, who would often call me the mayor of Providence, turned and said, "You truly are the mayor of Providence, is there anyone you don't know?" I grew up across the river in East Hartford, and yes, I knew everybody!

My firm was coming off a trying winter. Some of our top people had been banned from the industry over 'Mutual Fund Timing' charges. It was a horrible time during what I considered a very successful career. Putnam was the first major mutual fund company in Boston to be charged in November 2003. I was hosting an Advest meeting at Universal Studios, Orlando, Florida, when the news came that Putnam was facing timing charges. Steve, another wholesaler host from Putnam, looked ashen white. He turned to me and said, "Your turn is coming, and the word is, "We're hearing that we look like choirboys compared to MFS"! I almost fell off my chair. *No way*, I thought. Then a little over a month later, at our annual mid-December field force meeting, an edition of the *Boston Herald* published, 'The timing wall of horror,' an article exposing our timing violations.

Panic spread among my fellow wholesalers that morning as the meeting began. "Go back to your rooms," we were told! Call your best clients and tell them 'what?' It was chaotic! I called one of my best client teams in the western part of my territory. It was tense as they pulled the news up on their computers. They appreciated the 'heads up.' Still, they said they would put us on hold until they figured things out and saw what their broker-dealer had to say. I had a Christmas meeting scheduled at the large UBS Branch on Franklin Street, downtown Boston, months before I knew the date of our year-end meeting, and I had permission to keep it. So now what do I do? I contacted my MFS speaker, Fixed Income Specialist, and Manager, Jim Swanson, who said it was up to me. I said, "I'm doing it." Yep, I was/am a lot tougher than I look.

As a former Marine, I was fearless. After high school, I went to Parris Island. Following that, I was an Electric Power Lineman working at the top of 40 ft poles daily, so you get the picture. I didn't fear much. I have also included a recent picture of me climbing 'the Wall.' I occasionally teach at a local high school, and one morning last fall, I brought a gym class of freshmen to the athletic field where the Army had set up their rock climbing wall. At first, they were hesitant to try to climb, so I went up first–in my seventies! Then one by one, they tried it.

Gym class, November 7, 2021, showing first-year students at a local high school how to climb 'the Wall.'

Yours truly, directly at the back of Staff Sergeant Brown

PLATOON 309

THIRD RECRUIT BATTALION
SGT. P. STRICKLAND
APRIL 1st 1964

SSGT W.A.L. BROWN

M.C.R.D., PARRIS ISLAND, S.C.
CPL. D. ODACHOWSKI
PHOTO BY, J.F. MAAG

6

Yours truly, directly at the back of Staff Sergeant Brown

PLATOON 309

THIRD RECRUIT BATTALION
SGT. P. STRICKLAND
APRIL 1st 1964

SSGT W.A.L. BROWN

M.C.R.D., PARRIS ISLAND, S.C.
CPL. D. ODACHOWSKI
PHOTO BY, J.F. MAAG

My first job out of high school as an Electric Power Lineman
for Hartford Electric Light

I stayed and thrived for 30 years as a Financial Wholesaler. Let me say, "You're not going to become a successful wholesaler just because you're tough or think you're a 'tough guy.' But you won't survive very long if you don't acquire some toughness."

We got into the foyer of the UBS building, and we instantly noticed copies of the *Boston Herald*; you couldn't miss them with the thick print headline and picture, 'Timing wall of horror and MFS.' Swanson gulped and said you're sure you want to do this. "Yes, no question!"

I was very nervous; I admit it, very. I bought all the copies of the *Herald* and took them upstairs to the meeting room, placing them in a pile alongside our meeting literature. I know it sounds like I'm trying to make myself look like a hero by relaying this event. I'm not! I didn't need to then, and I don't need to now, but if you're a wholesaler, you've got to show up in good times and bad. I always showed up! Many of my competitors didn't; some went into hiding. I reaped the rewards of that statement and their lack of courage. I'll mention this again later on, **'First Rule of Wholesaling. 'SHOW UP!'**

The meeting at UBS went so, so. I think the advisors were as numb and dumbfounded as I was. It was the first meeting by anyone at MFS after the Timing Debacle, and I think I gave my colleagues the courage to press on. Despite all my meetings and efforts, business suffered soon after the news broke. Although management just wanted results, some forgot about what happened, and some pretended it didn't happen000000000. You knew it was serious when some of the senior guys resigned. (*If you're a college grad seeking a financial career, you will learn that even large companies can make mistakes and still be a great place to work once they have settled.*)

Chapter II

2000, Landing a $40million Mutual Fund Trade!

Since joining the MFS as a wholesaler in January 1987, I was either number one, two, or three (mainly one). I inherited an established territory with our corporate headquarters in its center. I did the job, but I also had access to everything and everyone in our home office. The year two thousand was my biggest. A consultant told me that according to the Investment Institute, Washington, DC, I was not only number one at my firm but also for the whole industry of 18,000 wholesalers. And I was competing with American Funds, which at the time allowed institutional fund sales to be included. That year, 2000, business was pouring in. Then I bid on a huge investment, $40 million, for a large organization near Boston. Their advisor had already placed about $ 8 million of their money with us, and everyone was happy with our performance.

I convinced President John Ballen and MIT Mass Investors Trust 1924 portfolio manager John Laupheimer to join me and help close the deal. I remember meeting them in the parking lot. John Ballen was the most outstanding money manager of the era with the MEG Emerging Growth Fund. John wasn't the best dresser, but they say,

'Clothes don't make the man.' There was a rip in the right pocket of his suit slacks, and I remember Laupheimer playfully pulling at it from behind. Unreal. Great fun guys, smart money managers.

I was fortunate to have them with me. President Ballen turned to me as we headed to the door and said, "Jimmy, what do you want me to say?" (I know what you're thinking. There are businesses where 3 to 4 days of preparation would be planned for such a large piece of business, not ours.) I replied, "John, go ahead and tell them about the firm, the fact that we were the oldest in the US, and mention our current excellent fund performance results. Plus, our current economic outlook." I told him, "I'd like you to 'close' with this." Tell them (members of the board's investment committee) to imagine that it's now 3:55 pm (the market always closes at 4 pm).

Further, have them imagine they/we just got word of a nuclear strike on China suspected coming from Russia. The future is unknown, but we know the stock market will tank severely. Then, ask them how quickly (they have 5mins) their stock managers (brokers) and bond managers will be able to sell all their stocks and bonds, of which there are hundreds, convert them to cash, and protect their investments? Then explain that one of the many benefits of a mutual fund is that in a minute phone call, you can tell MFS to move every penny to cash! Just before 4 pm, when the market closes!

He did it! Not as dramatic as I suggested, but close. Also a little more professional than my off-the-cuff 'close.' John Laupheimer followed with his best presentation of MIT. Mass Investors Trust, America's oldest fund from 1924. That afternoon the beginning trades from the $ 50 million began to trickle in. By 4 pm, the total trade of $40million was complete. I received the most extensive retail mutual fund trade in the firm's history!

Chapter III

Hartford, Merrill Meeting Continues, Possible Sale of MFS

Some Merrill advisors began trickling into the restaurant, but we needed to have their manager Jill Packard come down before we started. Jill was one of my favorite managers. She and another female Merrill Lynch Manager, Michelle Perrault, were among my biggest supporters. I had many supporters all over New England.

Portfolio Manager Thomas Melendez suddenly blurted out something about what I was going to be doing with all my money? "What are you talking about?," says I. He said, "Well, you own MFS Private Stock, don't you?". Yeah? "Well, CEO Rob Manning is meeting with the Chairman of Sun Life, our parent company, right about now." Sun Life was still upset about the firm's involvement with the 'Timing Crisis' and the subsequent firing of some of our top people in late 2003. They wanted to sell us! Doing some quick calculations, it seemed my stock could be worth $4 or $5 million. *Are you kidding me?* I thought. I had never drunk before any of my meetings, but I immediately ordered a scotch to calm me down.

He then said, "Most likely, the new owner would want to ensure that a guy like me stuck around and probably would offer a bonus that may be worth a million." I felt like I was beginning to feel dizzy. That was all too much after the previous nine months.

Chapter IV

Large Nav Trades, 'Making Money With Monks'

Speaking of large trades, especially before we got going with our 401k business and later with Separate Accounts, I made it a point to plant seeds about Net Asset Value trades (NAV) with brokers who I knew controlled some vast accounts. NAV allowed us to pay the advisor 1% and a .25 Trailing commission while not charging the client if they placed a million dollars or more with us. The commission was taken out of our corporate profits; so, great for their clients. In the mid- 1990s, an advisor at Kidder Peabody (RIP Mike) said, "he had an Abbot of a large Monastery for an order of Monks coming into town." He said, "The Abbot oversaw $ 12 million in investments for the order (Inappropriate to give its name, although it was a big one) and had a separate stock broker for stocks and one for bonds."

With a referral from a religious contact in Boston, Mike asked if I would present my NAV idea to the visiting Abbot. We met on the 23rd floor in a private room at MFS in our Boylston Street headquarters. Jeff Shames, president of MFS, popped in and asked if I needed help. I thanked him and said I was fine. I also naively thought it could affect the sale because Jeff was Jewish, and I was presenting to a Catholic Abbot. Thinking back, that was ludicrous. I just knew deep down that I was the one who could get the sale. Bottom line, I gave my presentation highlighting 'organization' performance (there were hundreds of stocks and bonds in their current portfolio), and with NAV trades. We paid the broker out of corporate profits. So, no commissions needed to be paid by the Monks. We showed better performance numbers along with our organized, readable monthly statements. I got my first large NAV trade of $ 12 million in a few days.

Afterward, with the help of our senior marketing manager (RIP Mike Russell), I set up a slide show including many of the other similar large NAV sales I was bringing in. We titled it 'Making Money With Monks' (pre-computers) which I presented to advisors all over New England and brought millions to MFS. Next, an advisor brought in the owners of a beverage distributor located in Mass. and who committed to putting in $ 1 million each month.

Then an advisor gave me about $20 million with a local college, and big tickets kept rolling in. These NAV trades were popular until the Separate Account Business became available. All this happened while I continued to bring in what I refer to as regular mutual fund business, meaning the $1000 and $2000 tickets I previously mentioned. My large ticket sales also acted like balloon ads. They accomplished the first phase in the sales process, which was/is the 'Attention Phase.' My firm and I got much attention. But I'm sure if you spoke to some advisors in Boston and other New England cities, they would say, "He never did anything for me, or he wasn't the best lunch presenter, certainly not as good as the Putnam guy or the State Street guy."

Well, as they say, 'You can lead a horse to water, but you can't make him drink.' You might think if you had access to a guy who brought in a Billion minus $10 million in a single year, especially if you were just starting, you might have him stop by your desk so you could pick his brain. No? I spent my time locating those I thought would listen to my ideas and luckily found enough. I was also available for weeknight dinners (I often stayed at hotels during the week vs. going home. Yep, it got difficult as my kids got older), not just to schmooze but to give ideas and create relationships. I didn't need the whole branch to love me, just a few! Most big mutual fund firms like ours always had at least one or two great performing funds, often more. However, I thought the key to my wholesaling success was 'marketing,' i.e., providing advisors with ideas for getting new and more business with my products and programs. For example, I had a generic hypothetical that could be tailored to an advisor's client I titled 'The Decade of The Seventies.' It was just a simple idea showing how well a client would have done by investing in our Total return fund and reinvesting dividends during the decade of the seventies when the stock market was flat. It showed clients making money due to the reinvested stock and bond dividends. It was a significant attention getter at my meetings. Some of my advisors personalized it, mailed it to their clients, and got hundreds of sales. The idea was so simple that many ignored it, yet others had great success. **Marketing was vital to my success! Equal to building relationships!**

Addendum: *I refer to some so-called coincidences in my stories and have witnessed many. In mentioning our Marketing Manager Mike Russell above, I recall my first MFS Christmas party at the end of 1987. As I was introduced to Mike, his wife came over, and he introduced me to MaryAnn. We stared at each other for quite a while before I remembered that she grew up one street from mine and was on my paper route back in eighth grade. "Was your maiden name Dobbins?" I asked. At first, she seemed bewildered and then said, "My God, are you Jimmy Naughton, from East Hartford?" We last saw each other 25 years earlier, in our senior year in high school!*

Chapter V

Acknowledging District, Branch, and Advisor support. Golf & Wholesaling

I had a decent expense account but tried not to be accused of buying business which I thought was, at the very least, no class. I probably lost some FA's, but that's ok. Politically, I needed to be liked by branch management. Some just cared about sponsorship and money for branch events, which I usually granted, but I think most realized I provided value to their FA's and branch bottom line. Some, like Merril Pyes, Manager of the large successful Boston Merrill Lynch Branch on High Street, initially wanted to control wholesaler traffic in his large 100-plus advisor branch. Early on, I was the only wholesaler allowed in his branch. I don't know why? Maybe because I met him when he was a young guy starting as an assistant manager at Merrill in Syracuse, and he realized that I was professional and sincere. Of course, I was just starting my career as a mutual fund wholesaler. You can imagine the jealousy this created in Boston over the years. There were times I felt there was a contract out on me. There was! Just kidding.

Early in 1988, I received a call from the Merrill Lynch Prime Plan Coordinator at the Boston Branch informing me that my luncheon meeting the next day that FA and Insurance Coordinator

Alex Jackson scheduled was canceled. Bummer, I thought, as it would have been my first branch meeting in the branch and took almost a year to set up. I had previously done 'walk thru's,' but I was looking forward to formally meeting everyone from the largest branch in Boston. The next day, while I remained in Providence, the Branch Manager, Vice president George Cook was meeting with a disgruntled employee in the room where my meeting was supposed to have taken place. Suddenly the employee pulled a gun and shot the manager. Despite many heroic efforts by advisors in the branch, he passed. The entire brokerage community of Boston seemed shocked as all highly thought of George Cook. I remember thinking I'll never complain about getting bounced from a meeting again.

Continuing my discussion on support.
Afterward, Paul Ferenbach became the Boston Merrill Branch Manager and supported me and MFS. Regarding coincidences ... Paul told me, as a new manager in the Midwest, his first advisor hire was Don Webber. Yes! He is the guy who hired me twice. 'Coincidence?'

It was always a pleasure to work with Connecticut Regional Director Fran Adams. His support helped make my career in Connecticut. Dan Mullane, National Sales Manager for Advest, District Manager Bill Cholawa, UBS Hartford, formerly of Advest, and Gabe D'amico, were equally helpful to my sales efforts in Connecticut. I will try to give credit to others in management later on. I also tried to have at least one intense center of influence in each branch. Paul Egan was that for me in the Hartford Merrill Office. He not only sold my funds but gave me marketing ideas. We would meet at the Goodwin Hotel for breakfast of their best Porridge any morning I was in Hartford. It wasn't like he was giving me branch secrets, but rather an idea of what the branch's focus might be that month or who the new FA's were. Paul never asked for a dime. He was a professional (an ex-marine) and recognized that I was also. While in Hartford, I always made sure to stop by and see Bill Greco and his team at UBS, one of the largest in the state.

In the early years, I had mutual fund/annuity coordinators in many branches. Advisors like Phil Baler first at PaineWebber (UBS), then SmithBarney. I would call Phil, and he would set up a lunch meeting with short notice. He did everything and always managed to have a crowd show up. So in about 30 minutes, I had a chance to present my funds and sales ideas to 40 to 50 advisors. I was fortunate to have the southern Connecticut Merrill Lynch District in my territory. Their Stamford District Sales Manager Frank Sullivan (originally from Rhode Island), had me as the lead wholesaler in all of his district promotions, which allowed me to bring in oodles of business. It didn't hurt when their famous District Manager Dan Donahue (RIP

Dan) told his advisors at my branch meeting that our MFS Total Return Fund was the first fund he sold as a rookie advisor. I was one of the rare few that had been given an 'open door' just about everywhere I went in the New England wirehouse brokerage community.

Attached is a complimentary letter from the CEO of a competitor firm that sums it/me all up as far as competition is concerned. Believe it or not, I tried to help everyone, including fellow wholesalers, as I thought there were enough investment assets to go around. I never did, and I suggest you don't talk ill of your competitors. That kind of negative style always comes back to haunt you/them, like Karma.

AllianceCapital

Alliance Fund
Distributors, Inc.
1345 Avenue of the Americas
New York, NY 10105
(212) 969-2176

April 19, 2001

Richard K. Saccullo
Executive Vice President
Head of U.S. Sales

Mr. James P. Naughton
Regional Vice President
New England
Broker/Dealer Mutual Fund Sales
Massachusetts Financial Services
500 Boylston Street
Boston, MA 02116

Dear Jim:

I had an opportunity to see the note you sent to George Keith on the rankings of our local wholesaler in the Northeast.

In a territory that is so competitive it was a nice compliment. The fact that you took the time to send your note says a lot about you and your personal qualities. It is no surprise MFS is our toughest competitor.

Very truly yours,

Richard K. Saccullo
Executive Vice President
Head of US Sales

cc: George Keith

25

Golf was a part of the wholesaler's life. For me, it was pure aggravation. I mean, I didn't like the game. Plus, I didn't like the idea of spending 5 or 6 hours on a course with only three other Advisors when I could be selling to 50. Some say it was because I sucked at it, which is true. I did suck at it, even after numerous lessons. I sponsored a golf outing for the Rhode Island Stock Brokers Association (headed by Dan Carney and Rich Dicharro, the largest producing broker team in RI in the era) at the RI Country Club in the late 1990s, which also included tennis matches. I sponsored many firm and branch golf outings. Always making sure I set up with some staff on a particular hole to be able to greet everyone playing through and subtly remind them who was paying. That worked out pretty well; however not as good as Eaton Vance's 'Hole In One' contest that their wholesaler Tony Robinson had developed. Then I would ensure I was around to schmooze at the cocktail hour following. I rationalized; thus, I talked to everyone instead of being stuck with a foursome for 4 or 5 hours.

I wasn't a great tennis player but a good racquetball player in college, so I figured it was better to play tennis than golf. I know I looked weird using racquetball swings and moves, but it worked. I was beating everyone. The highlight and the final match to determine a tournament champion turned out to be me vs. the American Funds wholesaler, Joe Blair. Probably the first tournament American

Funds ever sponsored. (They simply didn't do that in my day.). They were my main mutual fund competition. Joe, according to one of his American Funds clients, apparently played in college and was favored to win by a longshot. (Probably intended to intimidate me, which it did.) My first serve wasn't the typical 'throw the ball up in the air 2 or 3 feet and swing on the way down' it was about a foot high pitch and a quick but hard short swing which sent the ball sailing about an inch above the net, fast. Joe looked stunned.

The golfing brokers had finished their day and walked by when they realized what was happening. (Two of the major mutual fund competitors squared off). I now had 3/4 of the wirehouse brokers in Providence watching. Talk about pressure. Back and forth, we volleyed. I didn't think about winning and felt good just knowing I was keeping up. And I was too into the match to feel nervous, but I'm sure I was. The score was tied (deuce). He missed my next serve. Then I swung with what I know must have been the weirdest looking swing! The ball looked out at first, but it was ruled in. Joe, a tall guy, dove at it but was too late. The ball glanced off the edge of his racquet and rolled in a spinning motion a couple of feet. It was over!

I won! Unreal! Yes, I beat the American Funds guy! Unbelievable! The golfers all started shouting my name and clapping. They liked Joe, but I was from Rhode Island. As MFS PM Thomas Melendez

always said, "You are the Mayor of Providence."
I probably couldn't do it again, but the stars were
aligned! An omen because I soon became number
one in sales in Boston, where he and his firm once
ruled. That all changed!

*BTW, If you are a good golfer and a reasonably decent
wholesaler, many doors will be open to you! However,
you will note that I didn't do too poorly not being a
player, but if I was a decent golfer? I will never know!
Most of us are born with some gifts. Just know them and
use what you have. I did!*

Chapter VI

Hired by MFS 1987 as an Annuity Wholesaler, Selling Compass Life, a Variable Life Insurance Product

Initially, I sold annuities for MFS Massachusetts Financial Services as I was previously the Northeast Internal annuity Wholesaler for Dean Witter Reynolds (now Morgan Stanley). When I started in 1987, they wanted me to launch a new Variable Life product (Compass Life) a little like an annuity, but this one allowed a client to accumulate tax-free! I had some experience with this type of product, and Merrill Lynch was selling their version, Prime Plan, out the door. No one In MFS came close to my sales. I was 'numero uno' in the US for MFS Compass Life until the IRS changed the rules about the same time I moved to mutual funds. And that was just after we stopped selling Closed End funds that were not performing well due to incorporated options. I didn't sell any but guess who had to explain their less than stellar performance. If you're new or soon to be, financial wholesaling has had pitfalls, and I'm not speaking of investment performance. You will need to work around them or drown. There are always obstacles that a Financial Wholesaler must overcome. It's just part of the job.

When I left annuities, they brought in an attractive, talented young woman, Jane Mancini, whom everyone immediately liked. Jane took New England by storm. And she helped my efforts as copies of our funds were in her annuity product. They were no longer tax-free, but tax-deferred is the next best thing. Jane quickly rose to management. She hired Wayne Effron and his brother-in-law, Jeff Demers. Jeff and I traveled with one another for a time, hoping to sell my funds and promote annuities. Lots of hard work, but fun as well. Jane eventually became our National Annuity Sales Manager. She is still doing terrific in the industry as Global Head of Business Development at BNY Mellon. After Jane, Jac Maclean was National Sales Manager for Annuities. Jac always produced some of the best sales ideas for the Annuity wholesalers.

Chapter VII

Wholesaling with 401K, Perils for a Road Warrior! 'The Merrill Meeting Finally Begins.'

Later on, the 401k business took off. Again I was more than fortunate to have the best colleague and later great friend Carol Geremia in the field, helping sell and set up 401k plans. She was not only knowledgeable. but also very affable. The best. Brokers and just about everyone loved her. Together we owned the 401k business in New England for quite a long while. Carol was a brilliant presenter and just a nice person. Our first case was for $ 10 million. I considered it a gift. It was. We drove all over New England together in the early years of 401k. One of our big plans was a ski resort in Vermont with other locations. In the late 90s, we had an update meeting with the owners. That afternoon I had also scheduled a meeting with a Smith Barney advisor in Greenwich, Connecticut, who was working on a $ 30 million retirement plan. As soon as we finished our update with the ski resort, we jumped in what my kids called 'the old man's car,' my '98 Lincoln Town Car. I mean, what do kids know? Hey, It provided us a very comfortable ride on what was to be a long trip to Ct.

Oh, oh! As we approached the Mass border, I saw flashing lights in the rearview mirror. Carol turned a white color like the snow outside as we both noticed my speedometer on 80! I pulled over and waited as a 6ft plus 'statie' approached my window. *Crap! I'm done*, I thought. Stupid, Stupid, "Hi officer, I apologize for going too fast. I'm up on business and got a distressful call from home. I was nervous for a moment and forgot myself, driving this big new car. I have never had a ticket before. I'd appreciate you considering that." He went back to his vehicle after mumbling, "80mph"! I'm a goner; I wondered if they would confiscate my car and take us back to the station? Carol and I didn't talk. He came back quickly and handed me a paper. Whew! I got a warning, Unbelievable! Thank you, thank you. We rolled into Greenwich about 3:30. Yes, she convinced the advisor to let her bid on his plan. Soon we got a huge $ 30 million 401k. Later, at about 8 pm, I dropped her off at the Sheraton Hotel on the Mass Pike in Framingham, where she had parked her car. That's how it was during the 401k era in the mid to late nineties. For me, it was a fantastic, historical time to be wholesaling mutual funds and now retirement plans. I wouldn't have got the case without Carol. No way! But she might not have gotten the chance to quote on it if I hadn't mentioned and pushed our 401k program at my branch meetings. It was truly a team effort.

Carol also set up her great retirement plans team. I worked closely with Steve McKay, one of them.

He is now Head of Defined Contribution at Putnam Investments in Boston. During quarterly plan updates for 401k clients, Steve was always amused by how I handled participants' questions regarding poor performance because, in a way, I didn't. He said, "I had a knack for casually moving on to the next question, 'just kidding!' Steve later hired Rob Thompson to work with me. Rob was like Steve, terrific. (He is currently Vice President, Retirement Services Division, Marsh McLennan.) So when I speak or brag about my success, let me state here that it wasn't just me, it was with the help of colleagues like Carol, Steve, and Rob, and I also always had the best internal wholesaler assistants. I will take credit for my foresight to realize how important they all were to my business and ultimate success. It also helps to have good fund performance.

Although my boss, Dave Milbury, instilled in me that advisors do business with you for three reasons, 1. 'They like you,' 2. 'They like you.' and 3. because 'They like you!' I found that although they might like you, they're not going to place a poor-performing fund in their clients' investment portfolio because they like you!. And no, I didn't always have the best-performing funds. During those times, I might've worked on staying visible only so that I'd be remembered later on when things turned. Maybe I'll pay and do a seminar. I might push MIT, our oldest fund, as having lasted through The Great Depression. Or maybe the Total Return idea I mentioned earlier. You need to be creative when your performance is below par. I always came up with something to survive when I had to. And I think they 'liked' me because I always came back in good times and bad. So as previously stated, the **First rule for new wholesalers-- 'SHOW UP!'** As the years went by, Dave Milbury would also say to my colleagues, particularly when we were meeting in Arizona, "I could drop Jimmy Naughton off in the Sonoran Desert, and he would come back with business." The thing is, I believed him!

My Hartford Merrill Meeting Continues
Jill and the rest of the Merrill Advisors finally came in, and we began with Tom's presentation. Unfortunately for me, after hearing the news of the possible sale of our firm I was lost. Of course, it never happened. Sun Life and MFS were persuaded to stay together. I mean, what could you do if your top money managers decided to move across the street? I would have to wait for another sale or hope the stock price would eventually skyrocket due to business.

Chapter VIII

Separate Accounts, Meeting with a 1000 Merrill FA's

What was holding us back? The fallout from the Timing Debacle and the fact we didn't have Separate Account products to sell. It was getting scary. I was requested to attend a large Merrill Lynch convention at The Innsbrook Golf resort outside of Tampa. I remember riding in a Limo with National Sales Vice President Bob Leo and MFS President John Ballen. John was asking how sales were going, and Bob mentioned our lack of Separate Accounts. John turned to me and asked my opinion as a wholesaler. I felt a poke in my back from Leo. I knew what to do. I told him we were dead in the water on the wirehouse side unless we quickly entered the Separate Account Business. Later that afternoon, I gave a quick sales pitch to about 1000 Merrill FA's. After that, I introduced John Ballen.

At the end of the meeting, Hartford Merrill Manager Jill Packard came over to the PA system. And she was as loud as possible when calling her wholesaler Jimmy Naughton to report to her suite for a cocktail party. Can you imagine MFS Management hearing that? At the very least, Ballen knew I had credibility when I gave him my advice. As I said, around 1000 FA's were gathered outside the main meeting room. National Sales Manager John Rhoades started asking my fellow wholesalers what they would do? To which meetings were they invited? Talk about pressure. I requested a couple of them to come with me, so maybe I could hide them for an hour or so. Funny!

After the timing incident, many advisors seemed to stop selling our funds. When I asked why I was often told that we needed to get approved for some Separate Account products.

Something clicked. I think Ballen did some soul searching because it seemed that soon after Tampa, Separate Accounts Director, Bill Taylor, launched our Separate Account products. The business picked up again, and my belief that sales of regular mutual business would follow came true. Not everyone (management) was pleased! I wasn't very political, and I privately thought, *tough S^#@!* I knew deep down; *It would come back to haunt me.* I'm pretty sure it did. 'Six of one, half a dozen of the other.' Keep your mouth shut, and watch your regular mutual fund business dry up. Or, as a successful senior wholesaler, gently push the powers that be to approve Separate Accounts which were, in that period, 100% necessary for a Wirehouse Wholesaler. Later a supervisor says, "Oh, so you really think you're the reason we got Separate Accounts?" I said, "Ask Bill Taylor, Head of Separate Accounts. I only know I didn't prevent it!"

Chapter IX

Awards, Induction Into The MFS Hall of Fame, and Chairmans Club

My sales continued to increase, and I was inducted into the MFS Hall of Fame and The Chairman's Club. At our end-of-the-year Christmas Field force Meetings, I was awarded a Rolex Watch each year over three years for being Wholesaler of The Year. I'm not a bit materialistic, so I probably never would have purchased a Rolex. Now my sons each have one. I grew up under limited circumstances in a housing project, so I was in a great position to realize and appreciate my good fortune. Plus, I was hungry. I didn't look at my awards with the attitude that I worked harder than anybody and deserved it. I just always worked hard since I was ten years old. Back then, I often didn't even get a pat on the back. I knew I was lucky to be with the oldest mutual fund company and working in a home office territory in Boston. That was enough.

You would often find me sitting in my car outside our building on 500 Boylston Street at 5:30 am with a Starbucks coffee, just thinking and planning. Sometimes I would meet PM Bill Harris walking up Boylston and drive him to Max Bardeen's Kidder Peabody office for a quick breakfast meeting. Bill was revered at Kidder Peabody, which became part of UBS. Other times we would drive down to New Haven and do lunch with Fran Adams, Merrill Lynch District Manager at the University Club, and possibly a branch meeting at the close. I was lucky! Yes, with all the talent I had access to, it's no wonder I did a ton of business.

The United Homes, yours truly on a scooter. As I said, I grew up under limited circumstances.

Bill Scott, President, 'Head of Distribution,' presenting me
with an award for my production in 2000.

Chapter X

1980 Hired by Dean Witter Reynolds as an Internal Wholesaler
This is how my Wholesaling Career got started.

Wall Street was coming off the decade of the 70s, which wasn't a great time for selling stocks. In the 70s, the market was flat with no growth over the decade. Brokerage houses were looking for products their brokers could sell. Then a company called EF Hutton decided to use a single premium annuity. Annuities mainly were used as a 'pay-out' vehicle in the Life Insurance Industry, but Hutton realized the potential of the tax-deferred growth feature under Sec 72 IRC. By applying an attractive interest rate (Rates were extremely high at the time), their brokers could sell a product with tax deferral benefits that could be an attractive alternative to taxable CDs and provide some estate benefits as well. Plus, it would have no upfront sales charge. The product took off like a rocket ship, and pretty soon, other brokerage houses wanted to provide their stockbrokers (now called Advisors) with an annuity product to sell.

In November of 1980, while working as a Consultant/Trainer for Metropolitan and as a manager for The Providence Journal's

Telemarketing Dept. my wife showed me a short one-sentence job announcement in the Boston Globe. 'Insurance Consultant wanted by NY Brokerage Firm.' My childhood friend and Sales Executive for Paul Revere in Boston, Jim Maloney, had recently told me that Wall Street firms were hiring Insurance Salesmen. I was interested as I was getting burnt out working two jobs, so I called the Ad's Boston phone number and spoke to Don Webber. He was National Sales Manager for Annuities and Insurance at Dean Witter Reynolds (Later renamed Morgan Stanley). I was invited to visit the Boston office and meet with Don and the Northeastern District Sales Manager, Jim Dwyer. Jim was Irish, bald with gold-rimmed Pince-nez glasses, and an ex-Jesuit. I admit that at first, I found him a bit intimidating. I felt like he looked into my soul. He remarked at lunch that my shoes didn't look enough like Wall Street shoes. However, I did notice that before we finished lunch, he was giving me tips on how to do the job of an Internal Annuity Wholesaler. That was a good sign.

We ended our first meeting agreeing that I should go home and discuss the position with my wife. Sharon was apprehensive when I explained that I could sometimes be gone a week at a time. It just didn't seem feasible at that time. At 10 am the following day, Don Webber called and asked if I had a chance to discuss everything with Sharon. I said yes and continued to say that, unfortunately, with three babies at home and all our relatives in

Connecticut, I didn't think we could manage all the travel, plus I knew nothing about Wall Street. I was about to end the call when suddenly a raspy voice interjected on the other end. "Naughton, Jimmy Dwyer here; you're not going to make any decisions right now. Ok? Tomorrow morning you will go to the Providence/Green Airport and pick up tickets for the 6 am flight to Laguardia. There will be a car waiting to take you to 5 World Trade Center." Jim Dwyer was silently listening to my conversation with Don. I said, "ok." I mean, I didn't feel like I had much choice. Sometimes things are just meant to be, no matter how I almost screwed myself from a fantastic career, as you will later read about. Do you ever wonder if certain life events are simply meant to be?

At nine o'clock the following day, I was sitting in a large conference room at 5 World Trade Center with the DWR Vice President of the Insurance and Annuities, Tom Peck. Within about 35 minutes, I was shaking hands with Tom and Don. I accepted their offer to be an Internal Wholesaler of Insurance and Annuities for New England and Upstate New York. As I stood up to leave the room, I saw the Statue of Liberty and Ellis Island, where my parents had passed through many years before. That was during the Great Depression, having left their native Ireland. My eyes welled up!

What would they have thought about all this? I mean, I didn't go to Harvard. I was an ex-Power

Lineman for Hartford Electric Light after high school, an ex-Marine that decided to go back to school at an inexpensive state college (Central Connecticut State-now a university) in my 20s. I called Sharon and told her I was now a Wall Street guy. She was silent at first. I didn't realize her widowed mother got laid off from her job in Connecticut the day before. Sharon invited her to come to live with us. Things just have a way of working out. I was earning less than $20,000 from two jobs and felt I needed to make $30,000. In my first year, I did $80,000, no question whether I made the right decision. I soon learned that my territory New England and Upstate New York was number 14 'last' in the annuity and insurance sales ranking. By the end of my first year, I had brought it to number one. It remained there during my tenure with the firm. Taking the last place territory was a gift. I mean, where could I go if I took the first place territory?

Chapter XI

My First Annuity Seminar February 1981

Initially, I had no idea what I was supposed to do. Tom Peck sensed it and sent one of his assistants from the home office, Tom Barefield, out to travel with me and show me how to do an office meeting. We eventually discussed something called a seminar which he said I was going to conduct in my territory. Early on, Tom accompanied me to a large convention in Syracuse, New York, introducing me to all the upstate New York brokers. I couldn't remember being so nervous. Of course, it got worse when I stood up to say a few words. And Tom poked me in the side, whispering that I looked like an Iroquois Indian. Oh crap, I had a dark brown suit on, but still strapped to my front lap was a sizeable tan cloth napkin from the dinner table. Oh no, what were the brokers thinking? I instinctively grabbed it, swung it in the air, and said OOps! Great to meet you all. I remember much clapping. Unreal! So that's how my wholesaling career started. *(Tom Barefield became President of Ohio National Life and hired my son as an Annuity Wholesaler) 'Relationships open Doors!'*

A month later, in February 1981, I was asked to host a seminar for a couple of younger rookie brokers in the DWR Burlington Vermont Office. (I believe at least one of them is still active in the business in Connecticut, Hugh McIlrevey) I agreed, but on the condition that Tom Barefield fly in from New York and do it with me. I wasn't afraid, but I had never seen a broker seminar before. Tom ended up having to cancel coming to do the seminar with me in Vermont, but agreed to give me a script over the phone. I felt that I was beginning to hyperventilate. Then I discovered that the President of Charter Oil Company, Aaron Hockman, was coming to speak at the seminar. Aaron was a friend of Alan Synder, an Officer and the Senior Vice President of the Insurance Division. Alan Synder reported directly to 'Stretch' Gardner, DWR Chairman and CEO). I met Aaron at the Burlington Vt. Airport. I drove him to St Alban's Vt in some heavy snow. The brokers had rented space at the Owl Club in St Albans. It seemed that we were at the North Pole. Not quite, but not far from the Canadian border. Once more, I was very nervous (I knew that night I needed to find a way to squash the nerves). I mean, I was brand new. I had never been to a brokerage seminar. And it seemed that in St Albans, they were all farmers; how would an eccentric New York lawyer and annuity company wholesaler be received by them, in no man's land, in the middle of a blizzard? As I introduced Aaron, a loud banging erupted above like a bunch of hard thumping sounds. What the heck? I finished my introduction, walked quickly to the brokers, and said, "We need to quell that noise wherever it's from." The Owls Club was an older wooden structure. As it turned out, it also had some racquetball courts on the floor above.

You have got to be kidding me! The brokers ran upstairs, and the racquetball suddenly stopped. Thank God and Aaron got a standing ovation! I'm never worrying again. I now had to drive him back to Burlington. It wasn't that far, about 35 miles, but it seemed double that due to a cold, snowy evening. Oh, oh, halfway back, I noticed that my gas tank was almost empty. I am thinking that *I'm going to get fired.* I'm picturing Aaron frozen in a snowbank and Alan Snyder staring at me, asking, "Why?" This guy is friends with my top managers and represents the biggest selling annuity in my territory. Do you think that we would pass at least one gas station? Yes, one, but it was closed. Mentally, it was one of my life's most extended, nerve-wracking car trips. Finally, I pulled into our hotel on fumes with my ulcer on fire.

We did a ton of business out of that seminar. The farmers, as it turned out, were quite wealthy. Aaron called me a week later and asked if I could help him find a property to invest in on the Rhode Island shoreline. I located a 10-room mansion in Narragansett for under a million in 1981. We became friends. I realized right away that I had best put together a good seminar and learn it and then teach my brokers. I realized that we put together a great seminar presentation in that era. Now I had to teach it to my brokers. This is how annuities got sold in the early '80s.

Chapter XII

Meeting With DWR's Number One Annuity Salesman in Rochester, NY

I next flew to Rochester to meet the largest annuity-selling broker in the firm. Anthony 'Tony' Nicoletti. *How lucky is this?* I thought. I didn't know when I was hired that even though I had the lowest producing region in the firm, at the same time, I also had the largest producer of single premium annuities. Maybe I can get him to convince other brokers that were initially hesitant and cautious about selling annuities to get on board.

I did a couple of seminars with him. With Tony, It was a family affair; his wife would always come help serve coffee and knit in the rear of the room. His daughter would often show up and help with the registration. Tony had been a Vice President at a local bank. So early on, he recognized what a great alternative the annuities were to CDs, not to mention a 4% commission. Tony brought in millions. Our rates were as high as 15% in those early years. Considering they were tax-deferred, you can see why they sold so well. Tony told me he was doing seminars almost every night of the week and some luncheons. He published a newsletter to let clients know when he would be presenting in their town.

I finally put together my own seminar pitch. Looking back, it was very corny, but at the time, it sold millions. You're probably thinking that selling annuities would have been a no-brainer. However, for seasoned stock brokers in that era, it took much selling on my part to convince more of them to get insurance licensed and to become like Tony Nicoletti. I was confident that doing public and client seminars was the path to success. I also believed I needed to train the brokers on conducting their own business because I could only be in their branch once a month if that.

Chapter XIII

Three Hundred Attend My 1981 Annuity Seminar in Scranton! I Receive a 'Battlefield Promotion'

A year later, Dean Witter requested that I handle three branches outside my territory. Pittsburg, State College, and Scranton, PA. Tony had told me about meeting the Scranton Manager at one of the firm's many conventions. His name was John Egan. Scranton was doing very little annuity business, but I seemed to hit it off well with everyone in the branch. I told Manager Egan of the success I was having in Rochester with his new friend Tony, and I followed up by having Tony agree to give him a call.

Within a month, Mgr. Egan agreed to set up a seminar for his whole branch. He took out ads in the Scranton Tribune and did major mailings to existing clients. Many called in advance to reserve a seat. It looked like we were going to have a large crowd. I got to the hotel meeting room about 40 minutes early and noticed two things. The room was set up like a music chorus room with tier levels rising to the back, which was fine, but there wasn't any easel for me to put up numbers. I called John at his office, and he said not to worry. He had a bank client across the street and that he would stop and pick up their easel. The easel looked like it had been destroyed in a bar fight, all held together with scotch tape and paperclips. (Think about PowerPoint and computers available today.)

No time to worry about it now. Unreal, but attendees were starting to dribble in, and we had to get ready. One of John's assistants whispered that there could be over 300 in the audience. I knew I wasn't the world's greatest salesman, but I always had a story. That night I asked everyone to imagine the year was 1492, and Christopher Columbus had just landed in Scranton. Then I asked them to imagine him depositing a dollar in the local bank at 5% Simple Interest. And asked what they thought it would be worth that night? In 1981, 490 years later? I didn't wait for an answer. I just casually said it would be-$25.00 and wrote on the easel pad. Next, I told them that another bank in Scranton was offering 5% compound interest at the time. Then I told them to imagine getting 5% compound interest while emphasizing that Albert Einstein said, "Compound interest was man's greatest discovery." (Someone later said that Einstein never said that?) Again asking what they thought the dollar would be worth tonight in 1981, getting 5% compound interest? Of course, nobody had a clue. $25,000,000,000 Billion!! I answered while writing it on the easel. That was an attention getter! I also pointed out that in an annuity, they wouldn't be paying taxes while in the accumulation phase, making that number even more significant.

Early in my presentation, I mentioned another special feature of the annuity. It was this: In the early '80s, if you put $100,000 into one, you could take out 10% per year, i.e., $10,000, and pay no taxes. It was referred to as 'FIFO, First in, First out.' In some ways, it could compete with a tax-free municipal bond, and its value did not fluctuate like a bond. We mostly compared them to tax-deferred CDs with some extra estate benefits. I noticed a small commotion in the front row when I mentioned this. It turned out that a prominent doctor and his wife decided I was not being truthful and did not believe what I had just stated regarding that benefit. Pretty soon, it seemed the murmuring started to spread through the audience. Oh, oh, I'm beginning to think I might lose them. I shouted, "Let me show you," and started writing on the easel pad with my magic marker. Suddenly it collapsed and crashed to the floor. *Oh, Great!* I thought. DWR Manager John Egan, a former Marine, stood up, a little in shock, and ran up to the stage. "What can I do?" He nervously asked. I said come on up and hold the easel pad. Here was John, red hair with a green suit holding the easel pad, and I was writing on it. John was on the short side and looked like an Irish Elf. At the time, it was nerve-wracking. Looking back now, I have a smile and am close to laughing. I mean, 300 people, and I'm on a stage about 3 feet off the floor looking at an easel pad held by the branch manager. At the top, they could see the manager's red hair. At the bottom of the easel, you could see his brown shoes. He was a human easel. I mean, thank God I wasn't fully able to comprehend the scene that was unfolding. I might have choked.

I was still new at this whole seminar way of marketing. For that matter, I was still new to wholesaling! The audience seemed to quiet down, and I was able to make some additional salient points. In the end, many came forward and thanked me for the presentation. John was pleased. When he took that ad, announcing the seminar in the Scranton Tribune, he shrewdly asked that they send a reporter to the seminar. They sent two with a photographer. The next day the Tribune had a picture of myself, John, and others with the caption **"300 Get Reynolds Tips For Quadrupling Money'.** Prophetically, you might notice the name on the brochure I was holding, 'Spectrum,' Massachusetts Financial Services Variable Annuity. In the article, Elin Pye is listed as participating. Elin was a wholesaler for MFS National Sales Manager Doug Wood. As you read, I became an MFS New England Wholesaler 6 years later, in 1987. The reporters copied every word of my presentation and printed it under our picture. Thursday morning, the branch phones started ringing off the hook with attendees wanting to come in and invest. I had to rearrange my flight and stay over through Friday to help with the business. The article mentioned me as a Vice President of Dean Witter, which I wasn't, but I ended up with what I called a battlefield promotion because John called my New York headquarters to tell them what a terrific job I had done the night before. Soon after, I was promoted to Associate Vice President, then Vice President.

Regarding the following picture: I intentionally removed my presentation. Compared with today's FINRA's and SEC rules, the '80s were like the wild west. We made up our presentations. No one checked them. If any of my readers want a copy of the whole Scranton Times article, You can go to my book website www.KeyPublishingCompany.com and email me your request from the Contact tab, and I'll forward you a copy as long as you NEVER, ever, attempt to use it with the public. Finally, yes, that was my natural hair back then, not a wig!

ANNUITY SEMINAR – Dean Witter Reynolds, Inc., 211 North Washington Ave., investment security firm, held an annuity seminar Thursday at the Downtown Holiday Inn. James Naughton, Dean Witter Reynolds vice president, spoke on annuities. From left: John M. Egan, vice president, Mid Atlantic Region; Naughton; Jean Briskey, operations manager and assistant treasurer; William Comerford, vice president, investments.

(Tribune photo – Olds)

300 Get Reynolds Tips For Quadrupling Money

May 8th, 1981
The Tribune, Scranton, PA

By PETE GRADY

There's always an audience when money talks. Money talked Thursday night at the Downtown Holiday Inn, where over 300 persons listened to a Dean Witter Reynolds insurance specialist explain the value of tax-deferred annuities.

James Naughton, vice president of Dean Witter Reynolds, the second largest

from the contract values on each contract anniversary.

The tax-deferred plan allows the investor's principal to earn compound interest, the interest to earn interest, and allows money normally paid back to the IRS on or before April 15 to also earn interest.

Naughton gave a startling explanation of the difference between simple and compound

Elin Pye, a financial expert with Massachusetts Financial Services, an investment firm dealing in managing money, explained the 10 options in the flexible investment program. She said six of them were in income funds and four of them represented growth stock funds.

One of the income funds, the

Chapter XIV

Seminars Everywhere!

I borrowed sales ideas from everyone. DWR had a wholesaler in Florida, Milt Padowitz, a great salesman and treasure of sales ideas which he readily shared with us. John 'Micky' Finn of Atlanta, an avid baseball fan from Long Island, passed out business cards with a picture of him in a baseball uniform. (John later worked at MFS as an annuity wholesaler in Atlanta). Remember, the first step in the sales process is attention getting! I had zero wholesaling experience, so I made sure I learned from the best. Also, it didn't stop there at the beginning. **My learning lasted till I retired.**

My largest office was in Boston. When its manager Steve Lozen heard about our success in Scranton, he wanted in and began scheduling several large seminars at the Marriott, Newton, Mass. Business continued to explode. Not to be outdone, the Burlington, Mass Manager, Bob Maloney, invited me to do a seminar in his branch. He mailed every client registered to his office. So many clients showed up that he had to call the Burlington Marriott across the road and get a meeting room where he conducted a second seminar simultaneously. We must have had about 200 total at each one. Imagine that! Next, Alan Moutran from the Hartford office wanted me into one at the famous Hartford Club next to the Travelers Insurance Company. This momentum carried all over upstate New York and New England.

Chapter XV

New York City added to my territory, Closing a $600,000 annuity sale with one of Dean Witter's largest producers who was not insurance-licensed

The DWR wholesaler in Manhattan resigned. Selling annuities in New York City was a bit of a tough job. Tom Peck said, "You can have it if you want it." I said, "Yes, I loved New York; all my cousins lived in the city, and I was there many times during the year while growing up." Many guys were intimidated by New York and NYC brokers. Not me; I thrived on the challenge. So I picked up NYC and Long Island. My first meeting was in John Olsen's branch on the ground floor of the World Trade Center.

DWR became Morgan Stanley (I last saw John on TV following the 9/11 Terrorist attack talking about how he and Ed Sullivan, Syndicate Manager, led a group of employees down 74 flights of stairs at 2nd tower; all escaped. (Ed was a manager in the DWR Burlington, Vt. Later he was promoted as manager of the prominent Boston Branch and moved to Manhattan as VP of Syndicate at the 2 World Trade Center). Earlier my manager and a great guy, Bob Dwyer, at Buffalo DWR, was promoted to head up Syndicate, a very profitable dept. for DWR.

After the lunch meeting, I realized the top broker in NYC, George Repper, was not in attendance, so I asked his secretary if I could meet with him privately. She came back and asked if I could come back at 4 pm. So that's what I did. George was a large, tall man, foreign-looking with a hint of an accent. I learned afterward that as a young boy, he had narrowly escaped the Auschwitz Death camp at the last moment by jumping behind a tree. He was a definite survivor.

He asked me to explain the annuity concept and how it was being sold. I brazenly said, "Why don't you give me a list of your CD Clients, and I'll make some calls to them? That way, you can sit on the couch and listen to my pitch firsthand to decide if it's something you can use. If you don't know me and are reading this for the first time, you probably think this is some sort of fantasy story. Believe me; this, in reality, is how it went. I always had big cajones and was probably a tiny bit crazy at the time. I knew one broker (only one), later, a wholesaler in Providence who died very young, who might have done that, but I'm afraid George would have asked him to leave due to his mannerisms.

On my third phone call, I spoke to a client with 6 $100,000 CDs George had set up for his grandchildren. I thought he was an excellent prospect, and he asked if we could meet. I think George was impressed, and we met in George's Office the following day for coffee before taking a taxi uptown to the building near Central Park and the Plaza Hotel on 47th street. George, noticing the look of awe on my face as I stared at the gold-plated walls and the armed guards stationed at various locations, said, "Don't be nervous; he is a former partner of the famous 1980s New York Diamond Dealer. Finally, we were ushered into his client's plush office. The client, whose name I will keep confidential for obvious reasons, greeted us warmly. I made my presentation, and we walked out with an order for $ 600,000 Annuities and $24,000 in commissions for George. (Which the Insurance Company paid out of their profits, not out of the client's investment). It sounds too simple, but that's the way it was. Yep, I was a hero again.

One problem, however, was that George wasn't licensed. But I was. Whew! In those days, we held the commission until he took the test and got licensed, which he did. Afterward, we became good friends. I met his wife, who worked with him, and I was invited to dinner at their Condo, which was connected to another part of the World Trade Center by an enclosed walkway in a building overlooking the Hudson River. On Fridays, they headed to their home in the Hamptons, and due to heavy traffic, they listened to books on tape, which got me hooked in those early days. (RIP, George)

Chapter XVI

Trips and recognition for my Sales Achievements at DWR, Plus getting Advisors to sell Whole Life Insurance Policies and Implement Estate Planning

RI Senator Claiborne Pell sent me a letter acknowledging my achievements at being named DWR Insurance 'Man of The Year' (I was actually named DWR Insurance Man of the Year). Later on, Sharon and I were sent on a fabulous week-long annuity convention to England along with Boston Branch Manager Steve Lozen. The trip was terrific. We even got to fly to the edge of space over Scotland on the world's fastest jet, the Concorde. We were greeted by about 2000 Danes and a band when we landed in Copenhagen. We spent the day doing tours and went back to our hotel after that. We were in the famous Grosvenor House across from the famous Hyde Park. There we celebrated Happy Hour every evening with Glen Campbell, Telly Savalas, and Charlie from Charlie's Angels. They were all staying at the hotel for an international charity golf outing. The band Duran Duran also stayed there for one night.

CONCORDE

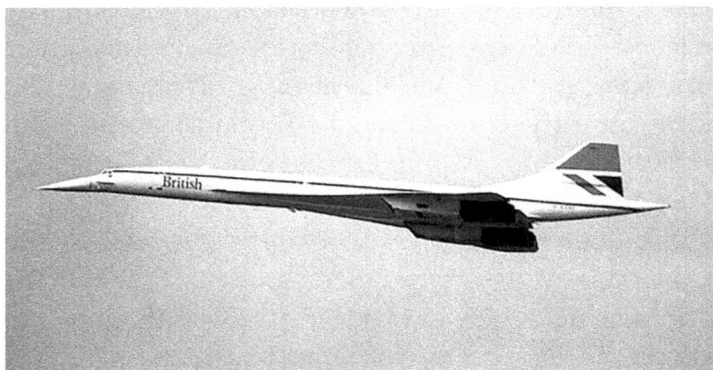

CLAIBORNE PELL
RHODE ISLAND

𝔘nited 𝔖tates 𝔖enate

WASHINGTON, D.C. 20510

March 24, 1983

Dear Mr. Naughton:

Just a line to offer my congratulations on your being named the 1982 "Man of the Year" and your selection as Associate Vice President of Dean Witter Reynolds, Incorporated.

This honor is, I am sure, well deserved and is a fine tribute to your enthusiasm and tremendously hard work.

With warm regards, renewed congratulations, and all best wishes for continued success, I am

Sincerely,

Claiborne Pell

Mr. James P. Naughton
50 Arrow Lane
North Kingstown, Rhode Island 02852

When I returned home, I met with representatives of the Hartford Insurance Company and Jack Friel of Connecticut General. Having already gotten my broker's insurance license to sell annuities, I persuaded them to be aware of potential Key Man situations for business owners. I suggested that their wealthy clients could reduce their estate tax liability with proper planning and life insurance. I was able to get some very experienced Life Insurance Consultants from those two companies to do most of the work and presentations. Trust was the most difficult as the brokers had to trust the insurance consultant I introduced to them with some of their more extensive stock and bond customers in that area. The Hartford and Connecticut General had the best highly trained, knowledgeable professionals. Yes, this project put yours truly under some pressure as well. As a wholesaler, I had to take risks to differentiate myself from the rest. When they started closing large cases of $10,000, and $20,000 with large commissions of 50% and more, word quickly spread, and suddenly I had senior stock brokers (now called Advisors) selling a large amount of life insurance with experts doing most of the work. It was a win-win for the client, the broker, and the branch. I was again a hero. (*If you're looking for a career and wholesaling seems of interest, don't concern yourself with a lot of the details I'm presenting here, I am confident you will be well taught in every aspect of the business.*)

Paul S. Bosnyak, CIC
Vice President, Divisional Sales

THE HARTFORD

1 Waterside Crossing
P. O. Box 320
Windsor, Connecticut 06095
Telephone: (203) 683-8158

October 16, 1984

Mr. James P. Naughton
Assistant Vice President, Insurance
Regional Insurance Specialist
Dean Witter Reynolds Inc.
42 Weybosset Street
Providence, Rhode Island 02903

Dear Jim:

A vote of thanks are in order for your great program in
"hyping" The Hartford and its' "Solution" to your life
sales force. It is not only refreshing but extremely
gratifying to see this kind of support from our colleague
in insurance sales.

Jim, I encourage you to continue to promote this creative
idea as I know it will result in a profitable relationship between Dean Witter Reynolds Inc. and The Hartford.
I look forward to the next update!

Respectfully yours,

Paul S. Bosnyak

PSB/ekw
pc: D. Drobnis
     S. Ellis

Hartford Fire Insurance Company and Its Affiliates
Hartford Plaza, Hartford, Connecticut 06115

67

Chapter XVII

Leaving Dean Witter Reynolds, 'All Good Things Come to an End'

Dean Witter was my favorite job. I made more money later in my career but did well at DWR. And I had fun; it's hard now to remember all my joy. I was treated like family, and whenever I showed up in cities like Buffalo, a car was waiting at the airport to bring me to speak at a branch seminar, usually at the Buffalo Marriott, to 50 to 100 guests. I loved it all!

'All good things come to an end.' Dean Witter got bought by Sears, who owned Allstate Insurance. My top guys thought they saw the writing on the wall and started to resign. Tom Peck was replaced by Phil Weeks, another terrific manager, and I got along with him famously. In any event, I thought it was time for me to move on, and I resigned. I still have mixed feelings regarding that decision, but I felt first and foremost that I was a wholesaler and needed to be in a company where I was the main conduit of that company's business. At DWR, my annuities were just one of hundreds of products. Still, it was hard to leave.

I saw the Worcester Manager Jim Higgins accept a job as manager of the Chicago Branch, a huge promotion and the backyard of Phil Purcell,

Mckinsey, and Co. Jim helped facilitate the sale of DWR to Sears. Jim was soon promoted to President and COO. Morgan Stanley. (RIP Jim) Jim and his Dean Witter Branch in Worcester, Mass, was my 2nd call after the Boston office at the beginning of my Wholesaling Career. He was always supportive of my efforts. Then my Buffalo manager and big supporter, Robert 'Bob' Dwyer, left Buffalo and took over the Syndicate Dept. at the World Trade Center. He was replaced by one of the best managers I ever met, Frank Perna, who was even more supportive of me and annuities. I had friends in all the right places. Again it made it hard to leave. I said earlier that I was treated like family at DWR. For example, after a few months at DWR. Jim Dwyer began asking about my family and how they were managing my travel. He told me he had a son a little older than my eldest son Tim. Jim felt there was no need to make a trip to my office in Boston. Instead, he set me up with an office in Providence 30mins from my home. Jim Dwyer's son, Patrick, became one of the largest wealth managers in Florida. I was privileged to give him a copy of my first book, *Jump in and start swimming*, in memory of his dad.

DEAN WITTER REYNOLDS INC.
#2 World Trade Center, New York, NY 10048

JAMES D. DWYER
Senior Vice President and Regional Sales Manager
Northeast Region

TO: Northeast Managers

DATE: August 20, 1985

RE: Jim Naughton

It is a melancholy moment when I have to announce the
loss of our good friend and insurance coordinator
extraordinaire, Mr. James Naughton. Jim is moving to
a new job with more responsibility, bigger challenges
and greater financial rewards.

Needless to say, we wish Jim well, double well, triple
well--during his five year tenure here he rendered
service above and beyond the call of duty. His personal
combination of integrity, product knowledge and hard
work, plus a winning personality, were the perfect
combination to win the hearts and minds of the whole
region. Result: a whole new attitude towards insurance products, oodles of business, and a multitude of
Jim Naughton fans. In this case parting is not sweet
sorrow, it is pure sorrow.

Jim has put our region on the map in insurance and
his shoes will be hard to fill, but fill them we will.
Please be patient, we will find another quality man to
take Jim's place.

cc: Jim Higgins
        Bill Shiebler
        Phil Weeks
        Dick Hayes

71

Chapter XVIII

Beginning a New Wholesaling Job

I was offered a wholesaling position with management responsibilities with my old boss and National Sales Manager from Dean Witter, Top Peck. Tom was among the most brilliant, decent guys I ever had the pleasure of knowing. He had left DWR to help establish a small boutique wholesaling operation called Omega services. Its goal was to emulate the success of the single premium life product Prime Plan sold exclusively by Merrill Lynch. These products were tax-free vs. the annuity, which was tax deferred. We would be offering a similar version and planned to distribute it to everyone else. Ownership was provided to me in addition to sales management responsibilities.

My team initially consisted of Brad Kohlstoe, Colorado, and Dave Tieman, New Jersey. On one trip to Brad's Arizona territory, while having lunch at the famous Peak in the Hilton Resort with Brad, we noticed a commotion at a table in the corner, a few feet to our rear. I sort of recognized the guy who came in with a baseball cap. The waiter confirmed it was Mike Love of the Beachboys, and they were putting the final touches on a new song, 'Kokomo' which they didn't end up releasing for a while. Later in the fall, after a meeting in our Long Island headquarters, we finished dinner at the

Garden City Hotel and went for an after-dinner drink at the lobby bar. Within a few minutes, we got waived to a booth on the far side of the bar. The group invited us to sing oldies with them. Unbelievably, it was Don and Phil Everly and their entourage. The Everly Brothers had just performed in Atlantic City and preferred to stay out of town, so they flew by helicopter into Garden City. An example of some of the fun wholesaling sometimes offered.

A year later, both Dave and Brad worked in MFS's Annuity Dept. Brad and Dave eventually went on to become wholesalers for significant firms. Our Variable Life product was too good to be true, so it required a lot of selling and education. My early insurance experience came in handy. The negative with the product was the question of how long the IRS would allow it to exist. I knew they had already taken away some annuity benefits. The company funding our efforts and providing the Life Insurance Wrapper was Monarch Life out of Springfield, Mass. After a year, unbelievably, they went belly up. Their stock plummeted one day from $97 per share to about .99 cents quickly. Fortunately for me, Massachusetts Financial Services was looking to launch their own Variable Life Product, making their funds tax-free.

VIENNA, AUSTRIA CONVENTION 1989

Left to Right: David Milbury - Former Senior Vice President,
Jim Naughton, Don Webber - Former MFS National Sales Manager

Left to Right: Tom Peck - Former National Sales Director, Insurance and Annuities, Dean Witter
Reynolds; Tom joined MFS as a Regional Vice President early '90s in Colorado, he is
currently an RIA(registered investment advisor), Don Webber - Former MFS National Sales Manager

More coincidences.

As I was leaving Dean Witter, my secretary Kay who previously worked for a Shearson internal wholesaler, also in Providence, informed me that her former boss Whit Whitaker (RIP Whit) had thrown his hat in the ring for my job. Even though we were both based in Providence, I had never met him. Within a few hours, I received a call from George Clary, VP of Security First Annuity Corp. (RIP George). George said he was in the midst of a problematic 'layoff' situation and had a newer member of his team, Jack Sharry, with a young family. And could I get him an interview? I called Jim Dwyer, and Jack was hired. Whit took an inside job with Eaton Vance as he said he didn't want to be in the field, which I never figured out (He knew something).

At the time, Eaton Vance seemed to be an old sleepy firm based in Boston. He was quickly promoted to National Sales Manager, and Eaton Vance became a very aggressive competitor. I say it all the time, "What a small world"! Years later, during a Prudential Convention, I met Whit at the Chatham Bars Inn, Chatham, Mass, on the Cape. He bought me a drink and said, "Do you know what a favor you did for me?" I replied, Yes, I do, and indeed I did. I told him it was nothing personal regarding my referring to Jack Sharry over him: it was just that I didn't know you, and I knew George Clary (RIP George) very well and Jack Sharry just a little, but I knew of him. Whit always would come over to me over the years and buy me a drink. He went on to success he never dreamt of in 1985! Fantastic coincidence or wasn't it? Jack Sharry went on to become President of Phoenix's Private Group.

Now at MFS, I was building relationships with every firm and every Advisor (no longer called brokers) all over New England. An announcement by my old firm, DWR, where I had so many relationships, hit me like a sucker punch in my stomach. Dean Witter Corporate Management decided 'external wholesalers' would not be allowed in their branches! I couldn't believe it; all those years, all those contacts. That's part of being an external wholesaler; you have little control. Many of my old manager friends 'looked the other way,' and I was able to work in their branches. However, they would be penalized if I did too much business! It was difficult. So I spent my time where I was wanted and hoped for the best. And it turned out the best!

The life of a 'Road Warrior,' as wholesalers were sometimes referred to, was not always easy. You had to deal with many obstacles if you were married with children. I ensured I always had a good electrician and plumber who would answer my wife's call quickly if necessary. I stayed in many hotels. Early in the 90s, on one freezing March night with snow still on the ground, I stood outside my hotel off I-84 near Danbury, Connecticut, shivering in my underpants, watching as firefighters put out the fire at my hotel. (I never told my wife about that one till years later.) From then on, I brought along a portable smoke detector, watched for and learned emergency exits, kept water in the tub, and always had a wet towel at the bottom of the door.

Soon after joining MFS, I had a meeting scheduled at Paine Webber (now UBS) in Burlington, Vermont. I left my house at about 7 pm on a Spring Thursday evening. I planned to stay at Ho Jo's in White River Junction, Vt., then drive to Burlington in the morning for a 9 am breakfast meeting in the branch. I arrived at the hotel at about 9:45 pm and unpacked my suit. I had traveled in jeans, a sweater, and new gray Nike sneakers.

Instantly I realized I had forgotten to pack my shoes. I called the front desk, only to find out that the only shoe store had closed early at 9:30. S*#t! Now, what do I do? I went down to the front desk and tried to buy the clerk's shoes which were about three sizes too large. He said, no! I decided to go to bed and get up early the following day, thinking *there had to be a store opening early in Burlington.* There wasn't! Nothing opened till 10 am. Here I was in a new gray suit with gray Nike Sneakers. I had to do the meeting. And it was my first time in this branch. It was too far a drive just to cancel.

I nervously walked into the branch, conscious of my sneakers, and followed the receptionist's directions to the meeting room, which was in disarray, with couches and chairs on top of one another. Were they getting ready to move, I wondered? So far, so good; the furniture kept my sneakers hidden. I was able to write on an easel pad hanging on the wall over a couch. The meeting started, and I noticed the manager sitting in front with a 'sour puss' look on his face. Great, I thought, at least he came. It went well until the pad slipped, and I had to step on the couch, exposing my sneakers to the whole room. I saw the strange looks from the brokers and tried to make it funny. I said, "Not only was I a wholesaler but was also an Olympic runner from Rhode Island,"; continuing with, "I ran up here"! Not a smile was given.

I finished, thanked everyone, and apologized to the manager for my sneakers. He looked at me with his sour puss and said, "You can do that once in this branch, you, understand?" "Yes, sir, I sure do!" Later that year, someone gave me a paperback book, 'Don't Sweat the Small Stuff.' It was all 'Small Stuff!' True, but in the moment . . .

Chapter XX

Selling Compass Life (A Variable Life Insurance Contract)

My first task at MFS was to help launch a new product called Compass Life that I mentioned earlier. It was a revolutionary product allowing investors to get into our funds and also choose from fixed Treasury Bonds, all growing tax-free under a small life insurance umbrella. When one took money out, it would be treated as a life insurance loan, so the withdrawals would also be tax-free.

Merrill Lynch had already begun successfully selling her version of this product called Prime Plan, so we could not sell our product in their branches. My insurance background, training, and experience with a similar product enabled me to sell Compass Life to my advisors easily. Along with Dave Milbury, I organized a meeting for greater Boston Bankers at the Ritz Carlton and began selling the product to banks in mid-1987. Soon after, with the passage of new rules that many knew were inevitable, the Treasury made the product less attractive, and eventually, sales halted. Again, all through my wholesaling career, I held a 'marketing attitude,' meaning I found uses and markets and then passed them along to my advisors. It worked. We went back to selling our annuities which were not all that competitive. Our parent company, Sun Life of Canada, was very conservative with our products' interest rates and benefits. We did the best we could.

After two years of selling MFS Insurance and annuity products, Dave Milbury promoted me to selling Mutual Funds. He said it's "the firm's bread and butter." Initially, this turned out to be an uphill battle as MFS got involved with using options to enhance the yields in some of their Government bond funds. Then they launched a bunch of Closed-End funds also containing options. As I entered my new mutual fund wholesaling position, advisors and clients began watching these investments tank, their NAV and price falling. It was a difficult situation. I wasn't sure how bad it would get. Who can forget Steve Esserig, our NYC Wholesaler, asking the 'powers that be' during our national sales convention how options were supposed to work. The speaker replied by describing the use of two buckets to illustrate taking money from one and placing it in the other bucket? Unbelievable.

Always the marketer, I began pushing our oldest fund MIT 'Mass Investors Trust' 1924, managed by our future president Jeff Shames. At the time, it didn't have the best performance, but I thought stability was needed, and here was a fund that started before The Great Depression and was still around, producing growth for clients for many years. I would say, "Do you think your clients want an equity fund with a 3, 5, or 10 yr record or one that's weathered the storm and had been around for more than 60 years"? My efforts didn't go unnoticed, and I received a congratulatory note from PM Jeff Shames. Doing branch lunch meetings in the early '90s in Boston was tough. Advisors were unhappy about our Government Fund and our dismal performing Closed-End Funds. Government means stability, not loss of money. Many remember the big crowds Milbury and I brought into the Meridian Hotel in Boston,'89, '90, and '91, for a pitch on our Closed End offerings. Probably not a good memory for some. My fellow wholesalers and I persevered. For me, the saving grace was that Merrill Lynch never let their advisors participate and sell them (closed-end funds). So I still had an avenue for sales with the largest brokerage house in America. It took a long while, but we began getting excellent fund performance out of John Ballen's Fund MEG (Emerging Growth Fund), followed by our other equity funds, including MIG, even our Total Return Fund, 'MTR.' Don't kid yourself; performance counts if you have recently started as a mutual fund wholesaler.

Being in a home office territory can be good when performance is positive, but it can be awful when it goes south. Speaking of the south, wholesalers there had some tremendous sought-after State Muni bond funds, so they were doing decent business while many of our colleagues were struggling. Great for them, but what about the rest of the country? District Manager Fran Adams from New Haven drove up to Boston on his own dime to convince our CEO Keith Brodkin (RIP Keith) to launch a back-end 'load,' Connecticut Muni Bond Fund. Fran even guaranteed a decent amount of business. Keith said within a week of Fran's visit, "no!" they are not profitable! Go figure. 'All is not fair in love and war and wholesaling.'

Chapter XXI

For College Juniors and Seniors — How To Get a Career as a Wholesaler (Plus a Day in the Life of a Wholesaler)

Remember, nothing stays the same. 'Can be a good thing.' Existing senior wholesalers may or may not remember, but from 1980 thru 1990, I knew of every telephone booth from Boston to Buffalo. Wholesaling without cell phones almost seems impossible now, but that's how things got done in the early years. Finally, we got car phones. Also, in the mid-nineties, MFS President Jeff Shames saw the need for us to get IBM Laptops and training. Both of these services changed wholesaling for the better, I believe. Today it's inconceivable to consider working without either of them. BTW. My first phone was a Panasonic, about the size of a shoe box when carried outside the car. Once inside the vehicle, it was attached to an aerial outside. A small transformer was installed in the trunk—all for $2500.

My phone was installed during a meeting I held at Kidder Peabody in Providence, RI. It became Paine Webber and then UBS. (UBS's Manager, Bob Gulla, was universally believed to be one of the best brokerage business managers and the largest producer of Compass Life.) RIP Bob!

Andy Bizinkauskas installed Panasonic car phones for myself and Dave Milbury while our cars were parked in the branch's underground garage. I remember because he eventually became a stock broker (as advisors were once called). Furthermore, his brother became a manager in a small boutique brokerage firm in Boston. Peter had me in often when he learned of his brother's phone installation story.

My day as a Mutual Fund Wholesaler (Annuity wholesaler also) often began with a branch breakfast meeting, generally with a smaller branch. (Occasionally, a prominent Boston Branch might have a branch meeting on a special occasion which I would always try to be a sponsor of). Getting in on one of these would often depend on relationships that I had established previously. Sometimes it was just a call and ask and get on the branch's calendar). At my breakfast and lunch meetings, I would present a particular mutual fund that management often selected as the fund or funds the firm wanted to promote at a given time.

I often used a projector to gain the attendees' (advisors') attention, allowing for a quicker presentation. I always looked for a story or a newspaper article that I could relate to whatever product or fund I might be presenting. It was my way of quickly letting my audience envision how it could benefit them and their clients. At the end of any branch meeting, I would mention that I would be available in the branch afterward and try to get advisors to ask me to stop by. I might have told them I had a unique hypothetical performance chart that shows the fund's performance for a chosen period using a dollar amount for the investment. Or that I had some other sales information I didn't pass out at the meeting. Or I would tell them of some special programs I was doing, maybe a successful seminar I held recently, or possibly success I was having, capturing 401k business to get them to ask me to stop by. I never liked the idea, nor did managers, of me walking around interrupting brokers haphazardly. During these after-meeting visits, I solidified getting some of the advisors' business and where I would ask for referrals from other advisors who might be interested in my products.

The breakfast or lunch meeting was just the attention getter. I always made it a point to stop by the manager's office to thank them for the meeting. I ensured they knew I had an expense allowance for major meetings or district conventions because I always wanted to be included. And I usually was.

I was fortunate to have a home office territory as I was sometimes able to get a portfolio manager to accompany me to the branch, or possibly Carol Geremia or Steve McKay to discuss 401k and later Steve Gessing for Separate accounts.

Doing lunch meetings was mandatory for a wholesaler. While breakfast meetings were not always guaranteed, I made sure I had lunch meetings scheduled four days per week. Of course, like with breakfast meetings, I worked the post-lunch meetings the same as I did at breakfast.

I tried not to use the branch for mid-meeting calls and paperwork even though many meeting rooms were empty. I had my 'go-to' offices at The Meridien Hotel, and operating from these improved my professionalism. Many who remember me know I was famous for The Meridien Hotel on Franklin St. (I believe the hotel's name might have changed) as I had its concierge park and maintained my car out front for easy access during the day and possibly evenings ($20, not bad for a big city).

In the evening, I often stayed at a local hotel, and I usually had a dinner set up or a ballgame to host with my clients (Advisors). As you read, I was big on seminars and tried to have at least 2 per week. In addition to all this, my branch and district sales managers were always running training or special meetings, which, as I said earlier, I made sure I was a part of, i.e., Sponsor and Speak.

There always seemed to be special events taking place. In the late 90s, some branches decided that they wanted to do client appreciation Saturdays. They would invite in all their clients and just about every Wholesaler, including yours truly. They would usually rent a hall and give us each a table to place our literature and gifts, golf balls, hats, and maybe a drawing prize. You might guess. We hated it! Could you envision how confused clients became after collecting literature for 7 or 8 mutual fund companies in a provided shopping bag? After a while, here in New England, it caught on like wildfire. Awful. It was eating into our expense accounts, and our wives weren't happy as we might have been gone from Monday to Friday, now weekends.

When a particular manager of a specific firm heard that so and so branches ran one, yep, they wanted the same. After one such Saturday event in Portland, Maine, all of us wholesalers decided to treat ourselves to dinner in one of Portland's excellent restaurants downtown. You had Joe Blair, American Funds, Nick Corvinus, Putnam, Tony Robinson, Eaton Vance, myself, and about four more from significant firms, all competitors. Someone suggested we throw our business card into a bowl and let our waiter draw, and whoever had his card drawn first would pay. So during dessert, our waiter said he would pull one of our cards. We all had pretty decent expense accounts, so in a way, there wasn't a big concern of a considerable out-of-pocket expense, but still. Probably a grand? The table became highly silent. Nick Corvinus, Putnam, the waiter, exclaimed, "card drawn!" Nick never skipped a beat, never showed any emotion. Pure class! After a while, we all said no, to the Saturday Client Appreciation events; we were busy. A very touchy situation.

In some cases, some guys were banned from the branch. That 'fad' eventually passed, thank God!

I thought there were a few questionable tasks, but otherwise, I loved it all. I enjoyed being included and helping an advisor attain his goals and the branches, districts, and firms be successful. I just liked being part of it all. I found that almost all of my wholesaling activities were exciting. In addition to increasing business for New England, I tried whenever possible to help our newer wholesalers. Sometimes it was company-wide email talking about the so-called 'Good Old Days' or sharing what was working in New England at one of our many get-together salesforce meetings. One of my proudest achievements was winning the Team Wholesaler of The Year Award at our year-end convention in Boston when I was presented with a Lapis Globe.

So how do you get a job as a wholesaler? I would suggest you get an entry-level position at a major mutual fund company like MFS-Boston, Putnam Investments-Boston, State Street-Boston, Columbia -Threadneedle - Minneapolis, Franklin Templeton-SanMateo, CA, American Funds/ Capital group-Irvine, CA. Use Google to locate a Fund Company near you. Insurance Companies also have Wholesaling teams for their annuity products. Your goal would be to eventually get a position as an internal wholesaler after at least a year of on-the-job and classroom training.

Maybe you know someone who knows someone. Or perhaps you will send your resume to one of the above company's Human Resource Depts. Be prepared for at least a couple of years of entry-level work combined with a great deal of training to learn about the various products and performances. At some point, you will also need multiple licenses, including Series 6 and more. During your first couple years, in addition to much training, you will get exposure to many careers and one of becoming a wholesaler. Stay flexible, and maybe you will discover what you want to do in this part of the Financial Services Industry. In the meantime, if you're still in school, I would take at least one or two speech and Public Speaking courses and possibly an introductory Sales Course if you're in a Business Degree Program, fine. I'm not sure what the thinking is nowadays regarding the type of major you have. But taking a few Business Electives might be helpful if you're in a Liberal Arts Program. I majored in English with a minor in Psychology. As you read, I went to work after college in the Insurance Industry, of which I knew nothing. They trained me! And my major didn't hurt my production numbers, as you read. Finally, I would consider joining Toastmasters if you have the time or after graduation. Do anything legal to set yourself apart! BTW. The pay is quite good!

Note: I published a College Job Guide for URI students. It is available on Amazon/books as an ebook. I might have some lying around the

house; if you go to my book website www.
KeyPublishingCompany.com you can email me
from the 'Contact Tab' on top, and I'll send it to
you if possible or go to Barnes and Noble for a
different perspective.

**Special note for college juniors and seniors
looking for a unique and lucrative career:** I have
placed an article from the firm's newspaper, *The
Reporter*, at the end of this book. It chronicles a
day in the field with me. Hopefully, even though
it's years later, it will provide you with an on-the-
job perspective. Things have changed and will.
However, the Financial Wholesaler will still need
to show up and discuss their products and make
an above-average income.

Chapter XXII

How My Early Career Prepared Me For Wholesaling

As you read this chapter, keep in mind that the preparation and training of a Financial Wholesaler had not yet been developed to any great degree when I began my career. Read this as it pertains to the history of wholesaling, not as what's going to be expected of you in today's era.

The following is some additional information on how I began my career as a wholesaler: I was trained in 1971 as a Group Insurance Account executive with The Travelers Insurance Company in Hartford, Connecticut, after graduating college a few years later than usual. I worked as an electric lineman after high school before deciding to go to college. (Nope, I don't think that job set me up for wholesaling except for feeling if you could climb and work up on forty-foot poles in the dead of winter, you could probably do anything. I believe my first career as a Group Insurance Account Executive was indeed setting me up for a career as a wholesaler. Fellow successful wholesaler and later MFS Head of Global Distribution Jim Jessee also started as a Group Insurance Salesman, so there was something to it.

Note: Jim and his brother Tom moved up to Boston from the Carolinas, where they were wholesalers and were promoted into management after John Rhodes, whom I worked for during the late 90s, resigned as National Sales Manager to become a Financial Advisor. A little earlier, Doug Bailey, our 'Up State New York' Wholesaler, was promoted to District Sales Manager for the Northeast. 'Example of the inner workings of a large company.' If you're still interested in a career as a wholesaler, just know you will have management possibilities as you progress in your career.

As a Group Account Executive with the Travelers, I called on independent Insurance brokers, holding meetings and selling them on placing our group health and pension products in their clients' businesses. Later on, I evolved into an Independent Agent representing not only the Travelers but other major insurance companies also. By the mid-'70s, I had gained experience selling all lines of insurance. Around that time, The Metropolitan Insurance Company had decided to change from the debit agent system and began selling Auto and Homeowners policies and whole life insurance. I was recruited with others to facilitate this change.

First, I traveled to all New England states, teaching their agents and enabling them to pass their state's Casualty and Property Insurance exams, allowing them to get a license to sell personal lines, Auto, and Homeowners. Once licensed, we would invite them to the Warwick Metropolitan Life mini-home office, where I would provide them with product knowledge. After that, I would present a Selling Skills Course. (The Warwick Metropolitan Life mini-home office was one of a few large offices set up around the country to reduce the operations in the New York City Homeoffice.)

It was here that I learned to present and speak in front of groups. Besides that, I had a speech course during my first year in college. I remember freezing like an ice sculpture when I first got up! My professor said, 'Do you know the Lord's prayer? Which I did. He then had me say it out loud. Afterward, he said, "Remember, if you know something, really know it, like the Lord's prayer, you shouldn't have any difficulty sharing it on a public stage like you just did." It was the beginning! I had the opportunity to listen to some of the best speakers in the industry and access many fellow wholesalers who were masterful speakers. I incorporated some of their styles with my own and did my best. Just remember, we are all endowed with certain gifts. As I have stated before, 'Use what you got.' You may never be the best speaker, but don't let that stop your success. Some of the best speakers I listened to never came close to my sales results. (BTW, your sales production determines how you get paid). Later in my wholesaling career, advisors, and clients said that 'honesty' came forward in my presentations. You can't learn that in school!

After a while, my family and I relocated to Rhode Island from Connecticut. The phone companies in that area were huge and looking to increase their revenues. I organized free training by telemarketing experts from the New England Telephone Company (One of the larger phone companies at the time). I provided telemarketing training to the agents and learned a great deal myself. I was very involved in all aspects of training and often went on sales calls with the agents in the evenings. One of my neighbors gave my name to Mike Dooley, Vice President of the newly formed Telemarketing Dept. for Rhode Island's oldest and largest newspaper, *The Providence Journal*.

The Journal had decided to sell newspaper subscriptions via the telephone with a group of telemarketers in 1980. I was offered one of two manager positions, three nights and a half day Saturday, while working full time at Met. I had been a newspaper carrier as a kid, where part of the job was to recruit new customers for my route. So the idea of doing it by phone intrigued me. It turned out to be a very successful endeavor. *The Providence Journal* received an award and was named number one out of ten thousand newspapers in the US.

It's different today. You'll not need a background like I had when starting. Generally, you will need a college degree to get an entry-level position. The industry has its own internal training programs. You will have an opportunity to look and apply for a wholesaler position, plus several other careers, including marketing if wholesaling isn't for you.

Chapter XXIII

Record Sales Late '90s – Great Performance, Large Nav Tickets, Retirement Plans-401k, and Separate Accounts. Plus the Best Marketing Programs. Plus years of Hard work!

At the beginning of this book, I mentioned how, along with superb performance, I came up with some great marketing ideas, i.e., 'Making Money with Monks.' Soon after, in the mid-1990s, I was traveling to New England with Carol Geremia selling 401k. Can you imagine getting your daily production report of individual tickets of $1000, $5000, or $10,000, and then a $ 20 million ticket from a 401k shows up? Talk about exhilarating. But that's what started to happen late in 1996. Early on, some wholesalers in some divisions decided that a 401k was not worth the effort. Unreal. Too bad for them! But that's how it was. **Take advantage of whatever programs, internal experts, and marketing your particular company has available.**

MFS had some of the best marketing programs. They supplemented all my wholesaling efforts. Often they alone could get me in the door. One of the more famous ones was implemented and run by Marketing Manager and Senior Vice

President Gerry Potts, 'Heritage Planning,' which helped advisors supplement their clients' financial planning goals. Gerry previously was National Sales Manager for our Banking Division. So he brought invaluable wholesaling and management experience into this program. We got advisors from all over New England into Boston for Saturday all-day workshops. It was a win-win, especially as our performance was heading way up! It was another way to schmooze during breaks and create new relationships.

We also had other popular field workshops. Senior Vice President Wayne Woodman, one of MFS's original wholesalers, would present Time Management and other sales workshops in the field in the later nineties. Wayne had a natural speaking voice with a hint of a western twang that in itself got my advisors' attention. Merrill Lynch Southern Connecticut District Manager Frank Sullivan often asked me to try getting Wayne to speak at various FA training venues. These marketing programs helped pave the way for me to come in later on and promote our funds.

By 1998, I was bringing boatloads of business, large Nav tickets, 401k, and our regular 'bread and butter' mutual fund trades. Marti Beaulieu, President of MFD, used my sales production at our Tucson Field Force meeting to show the positive effect on MFS earnings due to the ongoing management fees realized from my trades, assuming business stayed on the books. It was a humbling experience for me as it was presented to all of my wholesaling colleagues, who were all very successful in their own right. Then MFS decided to offer investment expertise in Separate Accounts. With all of this in the early 2000s, I was able to bring in almost a Billion Dollars, making me 'Numero Uno' in an industry of 18,000 wholesalers (Actually, it was $ 10 million short of a Billion, 'sort of.' I had $ 10 million waiting to be processed for a 401k, but it came over on Jan 2nd. Instead of getting it pushed through, I got a call from a member of management, not congratulating me on a good year but rather a great year – adding a reminder that it wasn't quite a Billion. Did your mother ever tell you about the 'Green Eyed Monster'? Funny now, thinking back, but can you imagine?

Chapter XXIV

Contributing Reasons For My Success: All of My Assistants, my Internals, and Company Product Managers

I said being in a home office territory when things were going well was the best. I always ended up with the best assistants and internal wholesalers. Starting with my first Sandy Horner (currently successfully wholesaling in Maryland), Terry Burgess worked with me next and went to night school for his MBA. Later on, he was promoted to portfolio manager. He is currently a Managing Partner at Wellington Management. Chris Grant was a terrific internal wholesaler. Some of my advisors didn't want to talk to anyone but Chris, even me! Chris and I were often picked to demonstrate to the field how to work effectively together as a team. Chris is now a Regional Vice President at BNY Mellon. Tim Chisholm, a Trinity Graduate, was an excellent Internal wholesaler for me. He is currently a Director of Retirement Plan Services at New Square Capital, PA, and Chris Logue, now Regional Director with Putnam Investments. Chris's father, former BC Hockey Coach, was friends with Dick Connolly, one of the largest producers at UBS and in Massachusetts. So I instantly had an 'in.' Imagine learning that Dick's mother was born not too far from mine in Ireland? On a family trip to Ireland, I promised to place my card on the mirror behind the bar of an Irish Pub in Dingle owned by Dick and a few other Irish Boston Financial people. I kept it!

Rich Gockelman was also my internal wholesaler. He is currently an Account Executive at Wolters Kluwer Financial Service and Solutions. Rich always made me look good. In the early years, I had 401k help from Carol Geremia and Steve McKay, who worked for Carol. Presently, Carol is President of MFS Investment Management and head of Global Distribution, while Steve is Head of Defined Contribution at Putnam Investments. Later, we promoted another of my internals, Ken Davis as a wholesaler in the northern part of New England. Kenny was an instant success. Steve Anderson of AG Edwards in Portland said of Ken, "Next to you and Milbury, he is the best that ever called on me."

Not to be taken lightly, Steve, in addition to being the top producing advisor in Maine, was number one in sales for American Funds. Ken is currently a Senior Regional Vice President for Columbia Threadneedle Investments, North Carolina. When I introduced Kenny to Steve at dinner, I said, "We need 30 mins of your time, and I promise never to mention a fund, only some sales ideas working in Boston. I also wanted to teach my wholesaling methods to Ken. So I launched into my 'Making Money with Monks' marketing idea and followed with a pitch on why he should prospect for 401 k.

It was a home run meeting; within a month, Steve submitted his first 401k case and became one of our largest producers. Kenny became one of our best up-and-coming wholesalers. Retirement Plans, and 401k, like separate accounts, got advisors to become more familiar with and sell our mutual funds.

After Ken, David Jodka joined me, working in Maine, New Hampshire, Vermont, and Boston. Dave was very talented and extremely smart. He got his MBA from Babson College while working for me nights and weekends. How do you do that? I barely made it out of a state college with a BA. Dave was brilliant, learned quickly, and became a good wholesaler. Plus, he was a great musician and band member. He took a wholesaling position with Evergreen Funds and later became Head of US Sales for Schroder. Sadly Dave, at 44, passed on, way too young, in 2014 due to a battle with cancer, leaving a wife and three young children (RIP Dave). Near the end of my career, I was fortunate to have Matt Crowther working as a junior wholesaler in Connecticut and more. Matt is now a Director for MFS in Conn. I also had John McDonough and Scott Matthews as internal wholesalers toward the end of my career. John is now Vice President at JP Morgan, and Scott is a Senior Business Analyst with our old firm MFS. I swear John and Scott knew me better than I knew myself. Half the time I went to give them urgent projects, they had already begun to do independently. My advisors said they felt like they were talking to me when they spoke to John and Scott. They knew how I thought and acted and sold accordingly.

I also had an industry Separate Account expert Steve Gesing helping me close deals. Steve started as a broker for EF Hutton and was promoted as a Separate Account Specialist before joining MFS. No doubt, I had the best, because we were a team. I included them in every aspect of my business. Colleagues like Steve and the others became my friends, so it was a terrific dynamic for even greater sales results. We also had marketing reps serving as liaisons with our client firms. Sandy McQuire covered wirehouse firms, so she provided invaluable work maintaining our corporate relationships and paving the way for me and my fellow wholesalers to be able to 'get in the door.' Sandy is currently Director, Senior Relationships Manager, Touchstone Investments. Again we were a team. I didn't do a Billion on my own. I took advantage of all the sales resources and individuals available to me. Imagine having this talent working with me as we rebuilt the business after the Closed-End funds and Option Government Funds in the late 80s and the early 90s.

BTW, every single one of them became successful in their own right. How could I not do a Billion in a bull market with the oldest mutual fund company in the US, plus all those products, the marketing backup, and excellent performance, with portfolio managers often willing to come out and present to my advisors in the field and more importantly all those internal wholesalers, junior wholesalers, and assistants? My apologies if I left anyone out regarding my praise. And, shame on me! I should have done '2' Billion! In my other books, I mentioned that one of my failures is that 'I don't think big enough!'

As stated earlier, I loved my wholesaling job at Dean Witter Reynolds, but it was MFS where I reached my goals personally and monetarily. I wasn't number one in any given year; I was 2 or 3, for which I was presented with a 'More Than Your Share' Pewter Cup at the end of each year for a total of 20. In the early 2000's I was given The Chairman's Club Award, followed by induction into the MFS Hall of Fame. I was awarded 3 Rolex watches for Wholesaler of The year, two of which I gave to my sons.

Now, I want to acknowledge my fellow MFS wholesalers from whom I learned and borrowed many ideas. Most of them received similar awards shown here. They were all professional, knowledgeable, and great wholesalers—the best in our industry. Writing about my experiences may begin to sound like I was the only one in the company making great sales. It 'ain't' so! It was team effort. That is why, I said, of all my awards, my Lapis Globe is my best, as it represents Teamwork.

Chapter XXV

Relationship Building

Note: College students need not spend much time on this chapter other than understanding how important relationship building is. Consider reading my book RELATIONSHIPS OPEN DOORS, shown below.

FA's like Barry McCloskey, a senior advisor at the Merrill Lynch Boston Branch and one of the largest producers in Boston, did not do much of mutual funds. However, he would let me know who was doing the business in the large Merrill Branch on High St, Boston. He would tell his team members to give me a reasonable share of their Fund or Separate Account Business when and if it was appropriate. With advisors like Barry, I would learn the branch and firm's focus, thus giving me the ability to know in advance what funds and products to promote alongside theirs. Barry would also call other large producer friends in other firms around Boston and tell them about my products. Guys like Kenny Zalcman, one the most significant producers at 53 State Street Branch. Bob Wyman, SMB Branch Manager, and his Sales Manager, Rich Green of that branch, gave me free rein to gain access and do pretty much anything I wanted in his unit.

Late in the '90s, with our entering the Separate Accounts business, more opportunities arose. I often met with Raj Sharma and his team at Merrill Boston after we entered the Separate Account business. Sam Cody, a close friend of Dave Milbury, was the same. He would do anything to help my efforts. Jim Joyce initially worked in the Smith Barney 53 State Street Branch, later at AG Edwards. Not only did he give me great business, but he also pointed me to friends around Boston. Paul Hartwell, a friend of Jim's, was another helpful advisor for me and fun! Maxwell Jumps! (personal story). Later I'd head over to Worcester. In the early years, I met Phil Neilan at Morgans Stanley. He helped me do business in his branch even though we were initially stymied there by their New York Home Office (Phil was a supporter going back to my beginning days as an internal wholesaler at DWR.

In western Mass, I called on the Keator Group in Pittsfield (now in Lenox, Ma). Sheila Keator was the matriarch, and her sons Matthew, Frederick, and David were a part of the team. They were in my territory, a pleasure to work with, and one of the largest of my MFS customers. They did more business than most of my prominent city advisors. Speaking of relationships, I met Sheila in early 1987, and soon after I began with MFS. On the way to Pittsfield, I'd stop in Springfield; Jimmy Guerra and his team at UBS in Springfield couldn't do enough for me and MFS by doing a lot of Fund and

401k business and setting up my branch luncheons. I passed through Providence on my way home and always dropped in to see Gary Venable, a senior advisor in the Merrill branch. Gary always had a trade for me and helped me penetrate the branch. He was very well respected by management. My wife Sharon and I became social friends with Gary and his wife Mimi, and he became my personal broker.

Next, I would head to Connecticut and have lunch with the Farmington Merrill Lynch Branch Manager Fritz Dahlgren. Later I would meet Jack O'Keefe, a former NYC KidderPeabody executive who would set up meetings at Smith Barney, Darien, Ct. In Danbury, Merrill Austin Drucker always gave me business but also directed me to FAs in his branch and his former branch, Smith Barney in Stamford. The above are advisors with whom I cultivated relationships over the years–sometimes many years, for example, Fritz Dahlgren, whom I met in 1981 as a new manager for the Elmira, NY, Dean Witter Branch when I was beginning my career. Another example is John O'Neill, now retired manager of Dean Witter (MorganStanley), Greenwich, Ct.

I sponsored and spoke at his first seminar with him when he was a rookie broker at DWR in Hartford, Connecticut, in 1982. John, Ed Sullivan, Fritz, and Steve Lozen were appointed by Jim Dwyer, who, toward the end of 1980, also brought me to Wall

Street and DWR. Mgrs. Jim Dwyer also appointed Bob Maloney and Frank Kale (RIP Frank). There are so many names like these that I owe part of my success in my wholesaling career. Some are 25plus year relationships.

Can you get an idea of the connections that came my way?

Relationships begin when you take some action, meet someone, and then get introduced to others they know, and so on and so on. How you grow them will depend on your goals and their needs.

All this begins when you leave your office and do something, anything, like a branch meeting, one-on-one with an advisor, or even a phone call. After seeing some success, some business, ask for a referral. Then, like a Miracle, things start to happen. A phone call, asking you to stop by; a seminar request, and on and on! Like Einstein said, "For every action, there is a reaction!" On the other hand, you can sleep late, stay home, and don't bother calling anyone, as no one is watching. BTW, I guarantee you will be back herding sheep in a few months, blowing one of the most extraordinary careers in the US.

What you just read relates to my second book, *Relationships opens doors!* (Amazon books). Also at www.KeyPublishingCompany.com

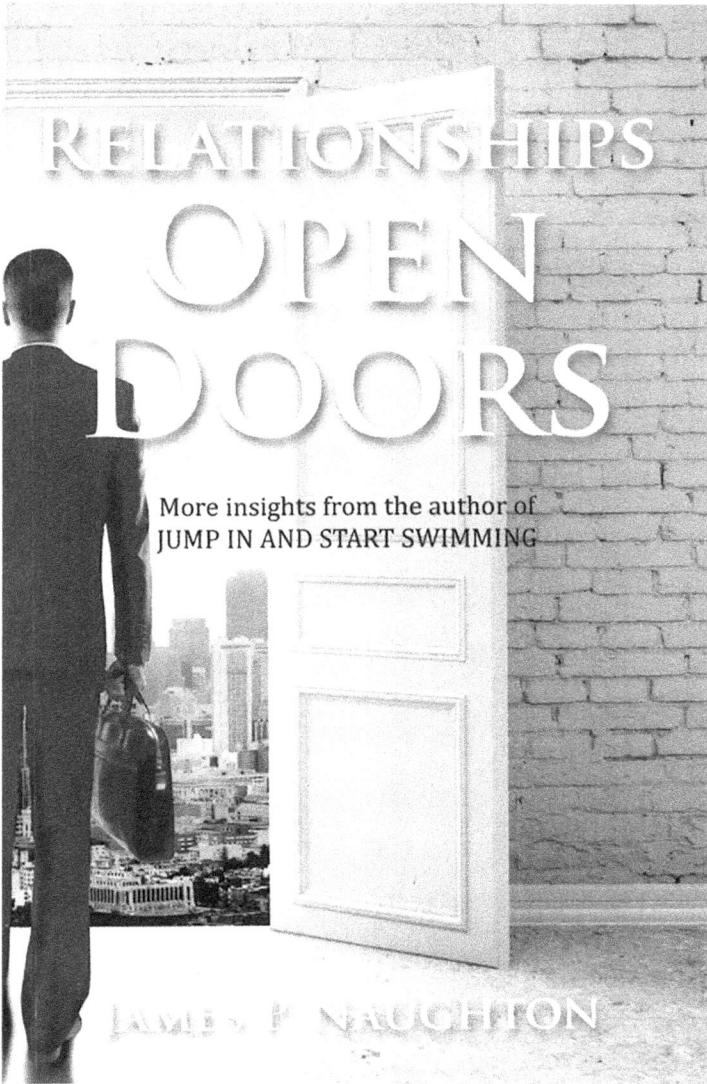

RELATIONSHIPS
OPEN
DOORS

More insights from the author of
JUMP IN AND START SWIMMING

JAMES F NAUGHTON

Chapter XXVI

Change

People tell me that things have changed. Wholesaling is different now. Yes, however, I realized that wholesaling was different every year of my close to 30-year wholesaling career and will change again this year. I have already mentioned the advent of our cell phones and laptops and how they changed wholesaling for the better. One of the most significant changes during my career was the terrorist attack on the World Trade Center, NYC, 9/11. That morning I planned on meeting with MFS wholesaler Rob Bonner in the AMC Theater Parking lot just off I -95, Exit 8, in East Greenwich, RI.

The plan was to drive down to Merrill Lynch in New London for a breakfast meeting and introduce Rob to the branch. Rob was in the process of taking over Connecticut. My daughter, Erin, yelled to me as I stepped out on our porch. "Dad, a plane just crashed in the World Trade Center." Thinking it was a small plane that mistakenly flew off course, I asked myself, *What is that idiot doing flying so close to those towers*? And then drove off to meet Rob. When I arrived in the parking lot about 15 minutes later, I noticed Rob leaning on the hood of his car. He looked pale to me. Something was wrong. When I asked him, he said, "the Tower is down." What the heck? What do you mean? He said it looks like there was a terrorist attack on the World Trade Center. I called the Merrill branch immediately and heard what seemed like a national announcement that all Merrill Branch offices across the US were shut down in an emergency. At that point, we could have been heading into World War III for all we knew. I told Rob to go home to his family. I did too.

After that horrible event, I could no longer walk into a building in Boston and get on an elevator to visit one of my branches. I now had to stand in line, so security guards could check my ID and call the branch for permission to let me in. Suddenly, I had to arrive about 40-50 minutes earlier than in the past. I also used to be able to show up at the Providence/Green airport and jump on a 'Bumper Jumper' flight to LaGuardia with only 15 minutes to take off and with little security. Suddenly you better arrive at the airport at least an hour or two earlier. As a senior wholesaler, I could go anywhere I wanted in Boston and elsewhere with very little notice. Now, it all changed – appointments, appointments. What's the future going to be like, people ask me? "Change," I answered. What's important is that you learn to adapt. Consultative Sales became a management mantra as they saw change coming. I think you need to keep an eye on 'marketing' you need to know where your products, and your firm, fit into an advisor's business.

Chapter XXVII

Some Additional Thoughts on Financial Wholesaling

I said I liked wholesaling. I know it sounds corny, but I loved it. Many guys thought I was crazy. I mean, they wanted the money, but not really the job. A little bit of me felt sorry for them. I don't think any of them sold life insurance door to door as I did starting out, except for our annuity Sales Manager Wayne Effron. That experience would have given them a different perspective, at the very least, I thought. I recall my third door-to-door attempt in a Manchester, Connecticut, apartment complex one Saturday afternoon, mid 70's. My first two rounds produced nothing except a couple of threats to have the police arrest me for trespassing. It was late afternoon, and I hadn't come close to getting a sale.

I knocked on the door for what I figured would be my last try. A guy in his late forties opens the door. I started my intro and pitch when he widened the door entry and invited me in. He told me he was a sales manager for a large paper company. Then he said, "Kid, I gotta tell ya, you're not gonna sell anything to anybody with that downtrodden look on your face. You must at least fake it that you're successful; start practicing a pleasant look, maybe even a light smile." Do you know what I did? I

117

never went door-to-door again. I realized that the days of Zig Zigler were over, at least in my neck of the woods. After that, I made an appointment, no matter how many phone calls it took to get one. The next thing I did was change my sales pitch. I began selling the cash value growth, a feature of whole life insurance (the interest rates were pretty good back then). So suddenly, in a way, I wasn't selling just life insurance, which at the time had gathered some negative connotations. I was offering a product with some consumer-pleasing banking characteristics and some life insurance that allowed you access to the cash value via a loan with no income tax charged.

One of my companies offered a passbook that you could mail in, and they would add interest similar to a bank. In wholesaling and life, try to come up with 'how to's,' ideas that would make 'YOU' personally interested and possibly entice you to purchase as you want your advisors to do. **Sell what your product does for your clients, i.e., 'Build a better retirement, set up an education fund.' Leave all the negative crap for your competition. Smile!**

I also enjoyed working for MFS and telling everyone it was the oldest mutual fund company in the US. It was an honor calling on Merrill Lynch and Smith Barney, Morgan Stanley, UBS, Prudential, Wells Fargo, RBS, Advest, and all of the wirehouse firms.

Chapter XXVIII

Discussing My Career with University of Rhode Island Juniors and Seniors

After retiring, I attended a wedding in Sonoma Valley, Ca. where I bumped into a former neighbor, Mark Crevier, an Adjunct Professor at the University of Rhode Island. Marc was also the CEO of a large RI Hospital. He lamented that his seniors were not getting jobs upon graduation due to the 2009 Economic Collapse and wondered if I would come in and talk to them and possibly create a 'spark' to help with their job searches. Mark knew that through life circumstances, I happened to have many jobs and careers in addition to my Wall Street Careers. When we got home, Mark contacted me and said the Dean of Business, Dean Higgins, wanted to be involved and asked if I would provide him with a copy of my 'talk.' I thought, *what was I getting myself into?*

I had already begun working on a memoir aimed at telling my grandboys how my career was. I also included information about how my parents immigrated through Ellis Island during the height of The Great Depression, discussing how they survived and thrived in our great country. After a month or two, Marc called to see how I was doing in preparing a speech. I told Marc that my 'talk' was evolving into a book, and I had combined my grandsons' memoirs. He said, "fine, finish it and well buy it." He also said the situation due to the Economic Collapse had gotten worse in that the parents of the seniors who had difficulty getting jobs were themselves getting laid off. Thus they had no money to pay the education loans.

Many have already forgotten how difficult things had gotten after 2009. I finished the book titled *JUMP IN AND START SWIMMING* after a quote my Irish mother would often use if she saw us procrastinating.

On March 28, 2012, I finally went to the URI Campus to spend a day giving 'talks.' As I arrived on campus, the picture below represents what one of the Campus Marquees was flashing. The others were exploding various events I was scheduled for my daylong visit. At 8:30 am, Dean Higgins met me in the parking lot, tossing a set of keys to me. He said, "Room 84, they're all yours, all 80 of my first-period students". That's how the day began!

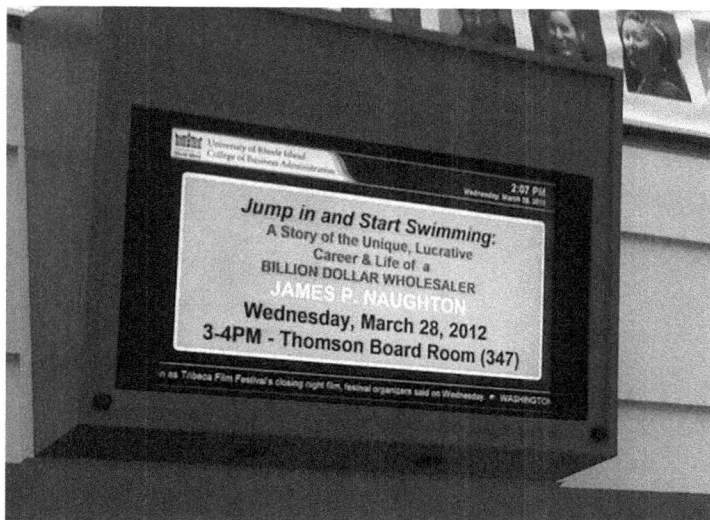

I gave two 'talks' to large groups of students, mainly from the Business Dept, and spent the time talking to juniors and seniors one-on-one. I was very well received. Interestingly, none of the hundreds of students I met that day had ever heard of a Financial Wholesaler, nor had they considered my industry's various jobs. Furthermore, I showed them slides of my after-high school job. I worked as an Electric Power Lineman. Also, I showed them a slide of the large electrical building supplies and warehouses I helped build after graduating college. (Myself, a former SteepleJack, and another college kid, Ford Diamond Electric, 6/2071) (Pictured further down.) Again I knew many careers, including the restaurant industry, newspapers, insurance, and banking, as I worked during high school at the largest Federal Credit Union in the US, The United Aircraft Federal Credit Union. And, of course, my Wall Street career. Afterward, students wanted more information on 'How I did, what did?' Many were intrigued with a wholesaling career, of which most had never heard. I knew from experience that one of the most important things they needed to learn and might not have gotten in school was how to NETWORK and build RELATIONSHIPS. So I wrote *Relationships open doors* (Amazon books) mentioned in the previous chapter for them and also a College Job Guide. I corresponded with many of them for almost a year. Eventually, most obtained a career.

Picture: Ford Diamond Electric, which I built with a former SteepleJack and another college kid beginning June 20, 1971, after finishing college. My boss Al said, "If anyone asks, tell'em you're a half-ass carpenter." Now it's 2022, and **it's still standing!** On Higgins Crowell Road, Yarmouth, Mass 'Cape Cod.'

Epilogue

Why now? Why did it take so long to publish this book? It's at least 5 or 6 years late. The most straightforward answer would be the Covid Pandemic, but that's only a partial answer. I began an outline for this book soon after retiring at the end of 2008. I simultaneously started work on a memoir for my grandboys outlining what I did in my career. As described in the previous chapter, I met with an adjunct professor who asked for my help. After I published my first book mentioned above, *JUMP IN AND START SWIMMING* (a combination of my grandboys' memoir and my careers), I began *RELATIONSHIPS OPEN DOORS*.

Between *Jump in* and *Relationships*, I thought they provided significant insight into my career, at least initially. So I began working on my *My How To Live Forever Series*, a project targeting my Baby Boomer generation. Amazon has waived the fee to upload an eBook for anyone. I realized there was an inexpensive way to publish a piece of their or their family's history and preserve it 'Forever.' If one were a President or a Monarch, it would be done for them. But the rest of us, 'nope!' I decided on writing five books or stories, as I like to refer to them, to differentiate that they are not literary works of art, just stories that we might tell our children or grandchildren. They would also have a teaching component, and the five stories can serve as examples. You could be preserving your story for your grandchildren, great-grandchildren, and longer by publishing it for free as an ebook. In any event, I recently finished my fifth story, *The Greatest*. The series is now complete.

I never thought the project would take ten years to finish. Unfortunately, I was involved in an automobile collision in April 2017; I was struck from behind while waiting for a light to change and ended up with numerous injuries, including a severe concussion with some short-term memory loss, all of which took a few years to heal. Then in January 2020, my wife Sharon went into the hospital for lower back surgery. Tragically she fell in the hospital bathroom the following day, fracturing her femur and injuring her hip and knee. Due to the Covid Pandemic, she couldn't get the rod removed and receive a replacement hip until February 10, 2022, two years after her fall. I'm not complaining, but I was her caregiver for the last two years. She was scheduled for January 6 this year at Brigham Women's, Boston, but it was canceled because there were 4200 hospital staff out of work due to Covid, an example of how bad things had gotten. Finally, the procedure was completed, and she is doing great.

In addition, with the risk of sounding like the 'Biblical Book of Job', last November, I was once again struck from behind while awaiting a red light to turn by a policeman (no flashers) who said a glare from the sun blinded him. I was knocked out for a while, and my car was totaled. We were both transported to the hospital. Yep, I sustained another concussion and numerous other injuries. I am currently healing. I know, you can't make this stuff up.

You have read that I traveled in an automobile daily for my job, 40,000 plus miles per year. How do you explain that my only 'offenses' were a few parking tickets? (Not counting that I almost had a 'ticket' in Vermont. And I was in an accident in 2017, due to no fault of mine.) Since, within 5years, I have been struck twice while stopping at a traffic light. Neither was my fault! I'm sorry it took so long to publish my wholesaling experiences, but I think you can understand. As they say, 'Better late than never.' I know times have changed, and many of my methods might not be as relative. *'But you must know the history to understand the present.'* So what I told you here is what I witnessed and did personally. And while I didn't do a Billion in sales every year, I was always one of the top leaders in sales since beginning my wholesaling career in 1980. I think this gives my story good credibility. What I experienced is significant and will hopefully help you if you're lucky enough to become a Financial Wholesaler!

You can reach me via 'Contact' on my books website ('a work in progress') www. KeyPublishingCompany.com. James P Naughton

One of my many retirement 'Well Wishes' This one is from a Merrill Lynch Branch Manager Christopher Bean.

CHRISTOPHER BRADBURY BEAN

April 2009.

Jim —

Glad we had an opportunity to speak this morning. You are one of the finest in the business — the consummate gentleman and professional. You have been a mentor and role model for so many of us in the financial service business. You always put the interests of your financial advisors first and knew that the business would follow — and it did. Thank you for always being a man of solid character and integrity. We always trusted you because you were always candid and always a man of your word. You are one of the legends in our business and I feel very fortunate to have had the honor of working with you and developing ⌇

a friendship with you. Our business will not be quite the same without you being part of it as you have been over these past 20+ years. You should be proud knowing how respected and loved you are — and how much we admire your son, Tim. Greatness runs in the Naughton family and your torch is carried with your son following in the family business.

I hope that we continue to stay in contact — a call here and there — and perhaps an occasional lunch and email.

I hope that I accomplish as much in my career and garner as many friends as you have through the years.

Best always. Keep the faith. Warmest regards,
Christopher.

This is the newspaper article describing a day traveling with Financial Wholesaler-Jim Naughton. The only thing it doesn't show is that it would have been very likely that instead of heading home, I would have been speaking at a public or client seminar that evening. Even though this was reported many years ago, I believe it will give a decent inside look at a day in a wholesaler's life. If you would like a Pdf of the article, you can contact me at www.KeyPublishingCompany.com

The Reporter · September 1990

Wholesalers bring MFS to financial advisers

The 57 wholesalers who travel across the country marketing MFS products will be in Boston October 1 to October 4 for their National Sales Meeting. Because we don't see them passing in and out of 500 Boylston every day, it's hard for many of us to know what the wholesalers' jobs are like.

To offer some perspective on the daily work lives and responsibilities of our field force, The Reporter sent John Lutz on the road with two wholesalers — Jim Naughton, who markets mutual funds to brokerage firms, and Jane Mancini, who markets insurance products to brokerage and insurance firms. Following are John's reports.

Jim Naughton helps New England brokers find new ways to market mutual funds

Wednesday, August 30, 8:00 a.m.
Meet Jim Naughton at Sheraton Tara in Braintree. Jim has driven up from North Kingstown, Rhode Island, an hour and a half away. Covering the eastern part of New England, Jim spends a lot of time in his car.

"I usually get up about 5:30 each morning," Jim says. "I like being able to travel by car. I focus on a given geographic area, and in a day I can hit a lot of offices.

"I think it's harder on the wholesalers in the midwest and west, because the major cities are much farther apart and they're constantly hopping in planes."

En route to our first brokerage office, we stop for coffee. "I worked late last night," says Jim. "I had a call night at a brokerage office in Rhode Island. On a call night, I buy a bunch of pizzas for the brokers in an office. First we talk about how they can market an MFS product, then we spend the rest of the night on the phones with prospects."

8:30 a.m. Jim conducts a breakfast meeting with 12 brokers in a Shearson Lehman Hutton office in Hingham. As the brokers drink juice and munch on danishes, Jim distributes

packets of MFS product literature and sales ideas. He first offers a broad overview of MFS products, then zeroes in on specific funds.

"Two of our MFS bond funds were recently ranked number one in total return in their categories. When you send a mailer with the number one on the cover, you can be assured of double the normal response rate."

For the second half of the meeting, Jim focuses on MFS Government Premium Account (GPA), using a slide presentation developed by Sales Promotion.

As the meeting closes, Jim notes, "Twenty years ago, total mutual fund assets were just $48 billion. Today total assets are $1 trillion. I think that's just the tip of the iceberg. You can sell mutual funds for a simple reason — people buy them."

9:10 a.m. The meeting breaks up and most of the brokers head back downstairs. A few linger with detailed questions for Jim. When all the questions are answered, Jim goes downstairs to visit the brokers individually. It's what the wholesalers call "desk hopping."

"I covered a range of products this morning. Now I want to reinforce some of the things one-on-one," Jim explains to me. While he desk hops, Jim has arranged for me to interview some of the brokers.

9:30 a.m. Meet with Bruce Henderson, manager of the office. My general question is, "What is the value of visits from a wholesaler?"

"Your worst fear as a broker is to be unprepared," says Bruce. "You never want to have a client ask you a question you can't answer. Jim gives us a lot of detail, but he's also good at presenting the information in an understandable way that we can use with clients.

"When brokers sit in on these meetings, they always have a client in the back of their heads. When Jim talks about a bond fund, for example, I'm thinking, 'Okay, maybe Mrs. Wilson would be interested in that.'

"Jim doesn't focus only on

products. He gives us sales ideas. Brokers are always looking for those. You constantly want a new twist on how to present a product.

"We've actually begun to limit the number of wholesalers we allow to visit. You don't want to ask brokers to take too much time away from their jobs of talking to clients. But Jim is always welcome here. He has an excellent reputation and makes a good presentation.

"We've had a lot of success selling MFS products. MFS inspires a lot of confidence among investors — it's a name they know and trust."

Jim's very good at crystallizing the information on all the MFS products for us.
— Richard Guillemin

9:50 a.m. Meet with Dick Guillemin, the office's mutual funds coordinator. Again I ask about the value of meetings with a wholesaler.

"At this morning's meeting, Jim covered a broad range of products. But for each one, he offered a driver, a key point that I can use to market the fund to clients.

"Jim's very good at crystallizing the information on all the MFS products for us. We need that. Just look at this," says Dick, pointing to a foot-high pile of mail on the corner of his desk. "That's just yesterday's mail. We are constantly inundated with information from firms offering investment products.

"Reading all the material would be impossible. We need to spend our time working with clients," Dick emphasizes.

"Brokers are the go-betweens between the sellers and the buyers of investments. What we need are one or two sales ideas that we can bring to clients. When we meet with someone from a firm, we want a story we can take to our phones and immediately use.

"I did just that this morning. I liked what Jim was saying about GPA. There were three key selling points he made. He mentioned that all the bonds in the portfolio were rated triple A or above, that it's a bal-
Continued on page 4

Jim Naughton

127

Personal interaction with financial advisers plays a key role in MFS' sales success

Continued from page 3
anced portfolio with both short- and long-term maturities, and that it offers an enhanced yield through option writing on a portion of the portfolio.

"I could pick up and run with that. After this morning's meeting, I came down and called a client I'm working with who has a $70,000 certificate of deposit that's just now maturing. He's coming in tomorrow with a friend, and we're going to talk about GPA."

10:30 a.m. In Jim's car, traveling to our next office, I mention that I was impressed with how many personal compliments Bruce and Dick paid Jim. Both kept saying "Jim's a good guy," a "decent guy."

"It's a fact of life in the sales world that people do business with people they like," explains Jim. "But you've got to understand what being liked means. It's not just coming in and telling jokes. It's developing a personal trust and creating an aura with clients that they're being taken care of.

"You build that over time by being honest with the brokers, by returning their calls and offering all the marketing support they need, and by backing it all up with good service."

"It's a fact of life in the sales world that people do business with people they like."
— *Jim Naughton*

11:15 a.m. At a Dean Witter office in Braintree, Jim's plans for a round of desk hopping are partially derailed because the firm's Internal Audit Department has made a visit.

Jim does manage to speak with a few brokers. In an informal conversation, he mentions the highlights of GPA. From the brokers he learns about new products being offered by other fund groups.

As we leave the office, headed for another appointment, Jim says, "That's the way it is with wholesaling. Your days don't always go as planned. Fortunately, today I have another meeting scheduled right after this. But sometimes you're left with a couple of open hours.

"You've got to be able to juggle things a bit. You don't want to let missed appointments throw you. If you can't spend as much time as you'd like in one office, you've got to improvise and get meetings somewhere else. You want to keep getting the company's name in front of as many brokers as possible."

Noon. At a Dean Witter office in Norwell, Jim makes the same presentation he did earlier in the day, this time over lunch. This is a smaller office, with fewer brokers. Six brokers have attended the luncheon.

With the smaller group, the presentation is less formal. The brokers keep interrupting with questions, so Jim's presentation becomes more conversational. When Jim talks about option writing on GPA, for example, the brokers want more information on how that works. Working on a blackboard, Jim breaks down the portfolio's structure and gives a detailed explanation.

After 45 minutes, the meeting breaks and Jim heads for a round of desk hopping. On the second floor of the office, Jim stops before the door of a broker who hadn't attended the meeting. The broker greets him with a curt, "What can I do for you?"

"Hi, I'm Jim Naughton from MFS."

"Oh yeah. I had a lot of success with your recent closed-end fund. Step in for a second. Can you tell me more about your Lifetime funds? I think I may have a client who'd be interested in a balanced fund."

For the next 15 minutes, Jim talks with the broker about the MFS Lifetime Investment Program, offering sales literature and answering the broker's questions about the Lifetime funds' management teams and performance records.

As we walk back downstairs, I mention to Jim that I probably would have been discouraged by the abrupt greeting and not tried to pursue a conversation with that broker.

"As a wholesaler, you've got to be a little thick-skinned," says Jim. "You don't know what the brokers' days have been like. They may have just lost a trade, and that's why they're abrupt at first. But usually it turns out to be a good exchange, as that one just was."

2:00 p.m. Before leaving the office, Jim pays a final visit to Bill McAuliffe, the office manager. I ask Bill the same questions I posed earlier about the value of these visits.

"There are a lot of investment products out there, but it would be too confusing to try to sell all of them," says Bill. "So we only let a few wholesalers in. When we do, I want a simple and clean presentation, and Jim gives us just that.

"Jim's also earned a reputation with us. We know if we have a service problem, we can turn to him and it's going to get fixed."

"My reputation depends a great deal on the support everyone at MFS provides."
— *Jim Naughton*

2:15 p.m. We head back to Braintree so that I can retrieve my car. I'll leave Jim as he plans to travel back to Rhode Island for an afternoon of desk hopping at offices in Providence.

As we drive, Jim explains Bill McAuliffe's final comment.

"There was a problem in this office with transferring accounts from another brokerage firm. I called Don Marra who had contacts at the firm, and with his help we were able to get the problem straightened out. That made my reputation at this office.

"You've heard a lot today about the importance of personal trust. I can't build that on my own.

"My reputation depends a great deal on the support everyone at MFS provides. That support includes investment management, marketing assistance and back-office service." •

Telemarketer Todd Charna (l) and Sales Support Representative Sandy Hornor. Wholesaler Jim Naughton keeps in close contact, via his car phone, with Todd and Sandy.

To my college readers: I hope I have made the world of Financial Wholesaling enlightening for you; however, I know wholesaling won't be everyone's 'cup of tea.' Remember that you will become aware of many other career opportunities in the Mutual Fund business once you get a foot in the door with an entry-level position. In addition to money managers, they need marketing managers, technicians, accountants, lawyers, artists, and many more in their marketing dept. And more. Good luck, and if you need to contact me, you can do so on my book website www. KeyPublishingCompany.com. Just click on the contact tab upper left. JPN

My Favorite Book: *For those I loved*, by Martin Gray. A Holocaust Survival story that I picked up and read over 5 hours on a Saturday before a Divisional dinner at The Plaza Hotel across from Central Park, NYC, early in my wholesaling career. I have always considered myself a survivor once I became old enough to understand the meaning.

My Favorite Quote: 'Always act like a duck – calm and cool on the outside, but paddling like a son of a gun underneath!'

For anyone interested in learning more about me and my early and fairly rugged background, you may want to obtain a copy of my recently published book THE GREATEST from Ingram Books, Amazon or Barnes & Noble. (You will need to type my name after the title as there are a number of "Greatest" titles on the market.)

JUMP IN AND START SWIMMING, RELATIONSHIPS OPEN DOORS can also be found there and on my website KeyPublishingCompany.com You can contact me from this site.

JUMP IN AND START SWIMMING,
RELATIONSHIPS OPEN DOORS,
WHATEVER HAPPENED
TO THE PECORDS?
HEAVEN SENT,
and
THE GREATEST
are stories from my life that I choose to preserve. Feel free to use them as a guide for your story!

To my fellow Baby Boomers: Write down a personal story or some family history and publish it as an ebook for free on Amazon Kindle.

To children and grandchildren of Baby Boomers: Encourage them to preserve a piece of their story forever!

"When the elderly die, a library is lost, and volumes of wisdom and knowledge are gone."
African Proverb

Price US$11.99

THE GREATEST

THE GREATEST
by the author of
JUMP IN AND START SWIMMING
(see back)

James
NAUGHTON

NAUGHTON

www.ingramcontent.com/pod-product-compliance
Lightning Source LLC
Chambersburg PA
CBHW071550040426
42452CB00008B/1129